SpringerBriefs in Economics

Kobe University Social Science Research Series

Series Editor

Takashi Yanagawa, Kobe University, Kobe, Japan

The Kobe University Social Science Research Series has been established as a subseries of the SpringerBrief in Economics Series, but in fact this exciting interdisciplinary collection encompasses scholarly research not only in the economics but also in law, political science, business and management, accounting, international relations, and other subdisciplines within the social sciences. As a national university with a special strength in the social sciences, Kobe University actively promotes interdisciplinary research. This series is not limited only to research emerging from Kobe University's faculties of social sciences but also welcomes cross-disciplinary research that integrates studies in the arts and sciences.

Kobe University, founded in 1902, is the second oldest national higher education institution for commerce in Japan and is now a preeminent institution for social science research and education in the country. Currently, the social sciences section includes four faculties—Law, Economics, Business Administration, and International Cooperation Studies—and the Research Institute for Economics and Business Administration (RIEB). There are some 230-plus researchers who belong to these faculties and conduct joint research through the Center for Social Systems Innovation and the Organization for Advanced and Integrated Research, Kobe University.

This book series comprises academic works by researchers in the social sciences at Kobe University as well as their collaborators at affiliated institutions, Kobe University alumni and their colleagues, and renowned scholars from around the world who have worked with academic staff at Kobe University. Although traditionally the research of Japanese scholars has been publicized mainly in the Japanese language, Kobe University strives to promote publication and dissemination of works in English in order to further contribute to the global academic community.

More information about this subseries at http://www.springer.com/series/15423

Narufumi Kadomatsu · James J. Kelly Jr. ·
Romain Melot · Arne Pilniok

Legal Responses to Vacant Houses

An International Comparison

Springer

Narufumi Kadomatsu
Faculty of Law
Kobe University
Kobe, Japan

James J. Kelly Jr.
Notre Dame Law School
South Bend, IN, USA

Romain Melot
UMR SADAPT INRAE
Agro ParisTech
Paris, France

Arne Pilniok
Faculty of Law
University of Hamburg
Hamburg, Germany

ISSN 2191-5504 ISSN 2191-5512 (electronic)
SpringerBriefs in Economics
ISSN 2520-1697 ISSN 2520-1700 (electronic)
Kobe University Social Science Research Series
ISBN 978-981-15-6640-0 ISBN 978-981-15-6641-7 (eBook)
https://doi.org/10.1007/978-981-15-6641-7

This Springer imprint is published by the registered company Springer Nature Singapore Pte Ltd.
The registered company address is: 152 Beach Road, #21-01/04 Gateway East, Singapore 189721, Singapore

Introduction

In Japan, the issue of vacant houses has rapidly become a "social problem" in the 2010s, and national and local governments have taken various legal measures to address it, including the enactment of the Act on Special Measures for the Promotion of Countermeasures concerning Unoccupied Houses in 2014. The problem of unoccupied houses is not unique to Japan, but is found in many countries. However, how the problem appears, what causes unoccupied houses, and how legal measures are taken to deal with the houses differ from country to country.

Land and urban planning laws in developed countries have traditionally focused on addressing the problem of "overuse" of land created by economic growth and urban expansion. In contrast, the vacant house problem symbolizes the "underuse" problem of land, which is brought about by declining economic growth and population decline. As a result, the basic premises of each country's legal system and legal theory will have to be re-examined.

However, population decline and a stagnating economy are almost always accompanied by regional imbalances. Therefore, the issue of unoccupied houses is seen as being linked to the regeneration of local economies and communities. When unoccupied houses are renovated and revitalized, it can revive the local economy. Even in a country like France, where the country as a whole has a growing population and has a housing shortage problem, dealing with the vacancy rate is still a significant challenge for local planning policies.

In addition, addressing the problem of unoccupied houses requires collaboration between the government sector, the market sector, and the public-private collaborative sector. A combination of measures will be required, including planning and coercive measures by the government, to stimulate the market in unoccupied properties and the management of such properties by local residents.

Chapters 1–4 of this book are based on the presentations at the international symposium "Legal Responses to the problem of vacant houses—U.S.A., Germany, France and Japan" held at Kobe University on February 12, 2017.

Chapter 1 (Emergence of Unoccupied House Problem in Japan and Legal Measures Towards This Issues/Narufumi Kadomatsu) examines the current situation regarding unoccupied houses in Japan and how they come about, followed by an analysis of the legal responses by local and national governments to address "unoccupied houses as a social problem." The chapter also examines the challenges that the problem poses to Japanese legal theory and legal institutions.

Chapter 2 (Municipal Responses to Vacant Properties in the United States/James J. Kelly Jr.) examines how municipal code enforcement departments, along with other governmental actors at various levels, respond to vacant residential property problems in the U.S.A. After providing a general account of the causes and effects of the vacant house crisis, the chapter focuses on municipal responses. It explains the inadequacies of traditional building code enforcement tools in preventing and abating vacant property nuisances and sets out what tools municipal governments need in order to respond effectively to the problem of vacant houses.

Chapter 3 (Expropriation of Vacant Property in France: The Case of Substandard Housing/Romain Melot) describes the general issue of vacant properties in France. It briefly reviews the legal and political positions on policy instruments to combat vacant housing, from incentive (public subsidies for housing improvement) to directive tools (requisition, expropriation). Lastly, the chapter focuses on an empirical study examining expropriation of substandard housing in the Paris region.

Chapter 4 (The Urban Planning Development Concept as a Central Instrument for Managing Apartment Vacancies in German Law/Arne Pilniok) focuses on the legal scheme "urban planning development concepts" in German construction law. The legal scheme comprises the essential urban planning reaction to the shrinking processes of cities and is intended to offer a flexible instrument for the municipal shaping of this transformation. This chapter points out that the legal scheme is geared toward cooperative and consensual administrative action and that one-sided action serves as a promoter of consensual action. It also points out that the execution of such norms is significantly determined by their integration into urban development funding by the federal government.

In addition to the presentations at the above symposium, this book also includes Chap. 5 (The Tragedies of the Commons and Anticommons in an Era of Underuse/Narufumi Kadomatsu). The chapter examines recent Japanese law's responses to the legal challenges of the "underuse" era, which is, as stated above, the background to the unoccupied house problem. It examines the legal issues of landscape as commons, area management, and the "unclaimed land" problem, from the perspectives of G. Hardin's "tragedy of the commons" and M. Heller's "tragedy of the anti-commons."

I would like to thank the authors of the chapters as well as many others for their assistance in the publication of this book. The above international symposium was funded by JSPS KAKENHI Grant Number 26301008 and also supported by the Kobe University Center for Social Systems Innovation. Yang Yashu (Assistant Professor, Osaka Gakuin University), Miho Uchino, Se NooRi, and Mikiko Matsumoto (Doctoral Program, Kobe University Graduate School of Law) assisted in organizing the above international symposium and editing this book.[1] Last but not least, I would like to express gratitude to Springer Verlag and the Kobe University Center for Social Systems Innovation for agreeing to publish this book.

Narufumi Kadomatsu
Professor of Administrative Law, Graduate School of Law
Kobe University Rokkodai 2nd Campus
Nada-ku, Kobe, Japan
e-mail: kado@kobe-u.ac.jp

[1]I would like to thank Editage (www.editage.com) for English language editing of this introduction.

Contents

Chapter 1
Emergence of Unoccupied House Problem in Japan and Legal Measures Towards This Issue

Abstract According to a survey conducted by the Ministry of Internal Affairs and Communications, the number of unoccupied houses in Japan as of October 1, 2018 was about 8.5 million, or 13.5% of the total number of houses in Japan, and is expected to rise further. Unoccupied houses are a problem in that they generate negative externalities for neighborhoods and inefficiencies for society as a whole, but at the same time, they may be a phenomenon that reflects some serious problems in the Japanese legal system, the economy, and society. This chapter examines the current situation regarding unoccupied houses in Japan and how this occurs, followed by an analysis of the legal responses by local governments and the national government toward "unoccupied houses as a social problem." Finally, other practical issues related to unoccupied houses and the challenges that the problem poses to legal theory and legal institutions are discussed.

Keywords Unoccupied house · Unoccupied house act · Perforation · Sponge phenomenon · Japan

1.1 Current State of Unoccupied Houses Issues and Causes

1.1.1 Current Conditions

According to the Statistical Survey of Residences and Land conducted by the Ministry of Internal Affairs and Communications, unoccupied houses in Japan as of October 1, 2018 total about 8.5 million, amounting to over 14.1% of all Japanese residences.[1] The severity of Japan's unoccupied house problem cannot be denied.

This is not to say that unoccupied houses in and of themselves necessarily always produce problems. If there were not a constant amount of unoccupied houses, people would be unable to move to new domiciles. The issues, we believe, are (1) unoccupied houses are creating negative externalities vis-a-vis the neighboring environs and social inefficiencies and (2) the high rate of unoccupied houses is not the issue in

[1] Ministry of Internal Affairs and Communications (2019).

N. Kadomatsu et al., *Legal Responses to Vacant Houses*, Kobe University Social Science Research Series, https://doi.org/10.1007/978-981-15-6641-7_1

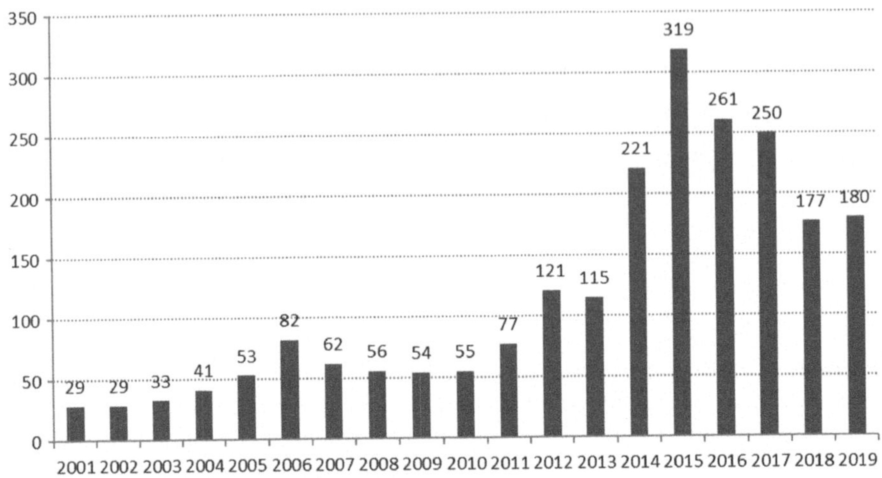

Fig. 1.1 Hit counts on "Kikuzo", the Asahi Newspaper Database (Search words: Akiya (unoccupied house) + Taisaku (measure))

and of itself, but rather that unoccupied houses are a phenomenon symptomatic of systemic issues in Japanese legal system, the economy, and society.

Let us first consider (1). When unoccupied houses are not properly managed, a range of issues occur. These include: (i) risk of damage from earthquakes and typhoons that causes collapse of the house or the roof or external walls flying off; (ii) hazardous pests causing sanitary issues; (iii) risk of fire or crime due to unauthorized entry by unspecified persons; and (iv) disturbing the surrounding landscape. Given that local residents have lodged complaints with their villages, towns, or cities,[2] the unoccupied house problem has gradually come to take on a new dimension as a "social problem."[3] As seen in Fig. 1.1, newspaper articles on the unoccupied house problem are on the rise.

1.1.2 *Causes of Unoccupied Houses*

We should consider (2) parallel with an investigation of what causes unoccupied houses.

Naturally, one macro factor behind unoccupied houses is population decline. It is estimated that the Japanese population, about 127 million in 2015, is doomed to continue declining. By 2040, the population is estimated to have declined to about 111 million, and by 2053, to about 99 million. By 2065, estimates put it at about 88

[2] Kitamura (2015, p. 56).

[3] Spector and Kitsuse (2017, pp. 76–77).

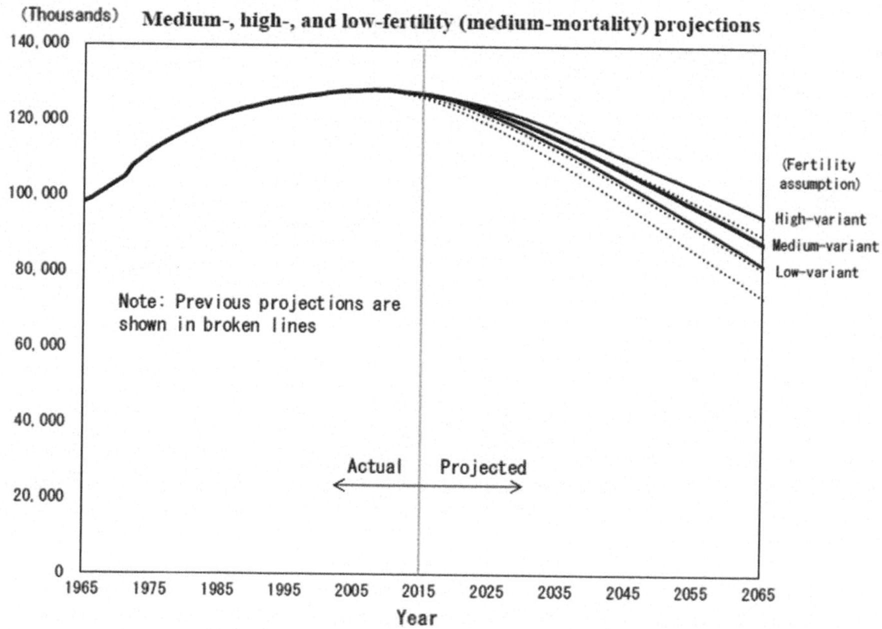

Fig. 1.2 Actual and projected population of Japan: Medium-, high- and low-fertility (medium-mortality) projections. *Source* National Institute of Population and Social Security Research (2017)

million.[4] According to these estimates there will be a 30.7% population decrease in the fifty years from 2015 to 2065 (Fig. 1.2).

While population decline may exacerbate the unoccupied house problem, it is not the primary or direct cause for the current problem. In the first place, population decline has only just begun, and given the rise in spouse-only households and single-resident households, while the population is declining, there are many regions in which the number of households is in fact increasing.[5] What we believe is exacerbating Japan's unoccupied house issue is Japan's foregoing residential policies, the conditions of the residential market, and serious problems in Japan's urban planning.

Japanese residential policy emphasized the quantitative supply of new dwellings and owners, a vantage point that came out of the drastic shortage of residences between the end of WWII and Japan's period of rapid economic growth. In 1968, however, the total number of residences nationwide exceeded that of households, and in 2013, the number of households was 52.45 million, with residences at 60.63 million. This has led to the country being referred to as a "hyper-residential society" (*Jūtaku Kajō Shakai*).[6] In 2006, the Basic Act for Housing was enacted. It

[4]National Institute of Population and Social Security Research (2017).

[5]Kobayashi (2016, p. 9).

[6]Nozawa (2016, p. 3). Much of what follows is based on Nozawa (2016, pp. 3–11).

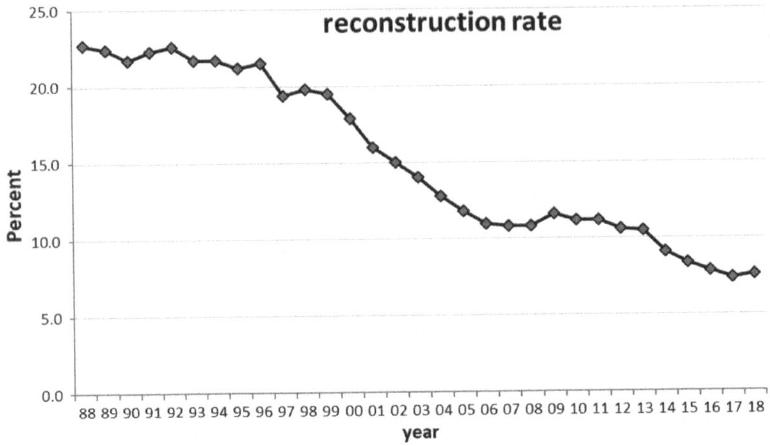

Fig. 1.3 Reconstruction rate of houses. *Source* Ministry OF Land, Infrastructure, Transportation and Tourism (2019)

was based on the idea of "effective use of existing residences," but the Japanese residential market's focus on new residences remains unchanged. Since around 2010, when the population began declining, the number of new residences being built nevertheless continues to increase each year.[7] The share of used residences on the market is on the rise (8.0% in 1989, 11.5% in 1999, 13.5% in 2008), but compared to the US(90.3% in 2009), England and Wales (85.8% in 2009), and France (64.0% in 2008), it is still very low.[8] Others have pointed out that the average lifespan of Japanese residences is 32.1 years (as of 2008–2013 average), which is considerably shorter than American houses (66.6 years) and British houses (80.6 years).[9] This short lifespan stands contrary to the fact that it is entirely possible to create wooden residences with a much longer lifespan of durability, given today's architectural techniques.

If, for the sake of argument, the residential market primarily comprised new residences and their lifespan were short, unoccupied houses should not increase if the existing houses are dismantled and new ones built on the same plots. However, this practice (reconstruction) is also limited, since 2005, to less about 10% of cases (Fig. 1.3). Put differently, 90% of newly-built houses are constructed in places where there had been none previously.[10] Deficiencies in Japan's urban planning schemes are the main cause of this.

Japan's current City Planning Act, created in 1968, treats its primary focus as curbing sprawl (the arbitrary expansion of cities), and it distinguishes between urban areas for focused development (Urbanization Areas) and urban areas to be adjusted

[7]Nozawa (2016, p. 4).

[8]Ministry of Land, Infrastructure, Transportation and Tourism (2013, p. 2).

[9]Ministry of Land, Infrastructure, Transportation and Tourism (2015, p. 35).

[10]Nozawa (2016, p. 11).

to curb development (Urbanization Control Areas), a form of zoning. However, the Urbanization Areas, which were intended to prioritize and systematize urban planning over a ten-year span, were in fact over-zoned to more areas. Further, this zoning was largely not carried out, leaving behind many areas with no development restrictions (unzoned areas). As a result, the 1968 law did not prove to be an effective halt to sprawl. With the spread of motorization, too, restrictions on the location of housing and commercial facilities declined, and cities sprawled further. Between 1990 and around 2000, policy reforms were made to expand municipalities' land use rights, but those municipalities located in the midst of competitive population and development growth areas were passive about stricter reforms. Around the late 2000s, the government began making reference to "compact cities" in its urban planning policy, and it reformed the City Planning Act, but this did not stop the arbitrary distribution of residences. As a result, new residences were built in ex-urban areas in which the land use restrictions were flexible, causing those extant dwellings in city zones to become vacant. This "hollowing out" or "perforation" of property and dwellings in existing city areas, is in recent years referred to as the "sponge phenomenon" in cities. In terms of maintaining and managing the infrastructure used to support urban life, this "sponge phenomenon" is producing major inefficiencies.

Next, let us consider, from the vantage point of owners of unoccupied property, why insufficiently managed residences appear in the first place. Let us say that someone's parent(s) die and they inherit the house in which the parent(s) lived. Even if the inheritor were to not use the house, no negative externality would be caused to the neighbors provided they (1) adequately maintain the property in question; (2) sell or lease the property; or (3) dismantle the property and create an empty lot.

If there is sufficient demand for used residences, (2) is possible. If there is sufficient demand for empty lots, (3) is possible. We have already discussed above why, based on Japan's residential policy and the market, these do not occur. By contrast, if there is no need for the owner of the property to bear the costs of negative externalities to neighbors, they have no incentive to continue managing the property in an adequate fashion. Therefore, the design of future legislation will likely look to place this obligation of expenses on property owners and internalize what are currently negative externalities.

1.2 Municipal and National Legislation Towards "Unoccupied Houses as a Social Problem"

1.2.1 Independent Ordinances in Local Municipalities

As described above, complaints from local residents have transformed the issue of unoccupied houses into a "social problem", and municipal governments have been called on to address it. However, the legal authority these municipal governments have is limited. The Building Standards Act defines basic rules on buildings. Article

10, Clause 3 of the law states that for buildings with "significant threat to safety or significant harm to hygiene/sanitation," the government retains the right to order their dismantling or "other measures necessary for the maintenance of safety and/or sanitation."[11] However, the requirement of "significant threat to safety or significant threat to hygiene/sanitation" is abstract, so it proved difficult to exercise these rights for these cases. Furthermore, all municipal governments do not have this right, so small-scale municipalities were unable to exercise it.

As a result, many municipalities elected to handle the unoccupied house problem by creating their own independent ordinances. In Japan local municipalities (prefectures, villages, towns, and cities) can enact independent ordinances and regulations without the express authorization of the national government. These independent ordinances exist as a standalone entity separate from national law. While they allow for stipulating orders, prohibitions, and penalties, where national law and a local ordinance are in conflict, the national law takes precedence.

In 2010, following an ordinance promulgated by Torokozawa City in Saitama Prefecture, many municipal governments (and some prefectures) issued a series of ordinances on unoccupied houses.[12] However, there were many limitations to how the unoccupied house issue could be handled by these independent forms of legislation.

First was the issue of identifying owners of these properties. Real estate registers in Japan indicate the names of house owners, but there are many cases where this name does not correspond to the actual owner. There may be cases where the new name after the sale of a property is not registered, or where the successors are unknown or too many, so that the contact with all of them would be unrealistic.[13]

Secondly, there were limits to the enforceability of the measures stipulated by these ordinances. Where an independent ordinance finds an unoccupied house subject to an order of dismantling, it can be forcibly removed by subrogation if the owner does not comply. While some ordinances do stipulate advice, guidance, and recommendations, they do not explicitly stipulate subrogation. Some ordinances stipulated the publication of the names of those parties not complying with administrative guidance.

Where measures for ordering disposal are in place and subrogation planned, if the owner cannot be identified, this cannot be executed. National laws such as the Building Standards Act may stipulate that, if an investigation fails to identify the

[11] In addition, in the case of "special buildings" such as theater, movie theater or business office of a certain size, the government may recommend or order measures at the level of the "risk" of significant threat to safety or significant harm to hygiene/sanitation (Building Standards Act, Article 10, Paragraph 1 and 2). However, we may assume that not many unoccupied houses currently considered as a problem belong to the "special buildings".

[12] As of October 2014, 401 municipalities have done so.

[13] "Owner-unknown land problem" has recently become a focus of public attention. The registration to real estate registers is not a legal duty in Japan. The land owners must pay a certain amount of fee for the registration. Hence, where the land price is quite low, there is no incentive for the new owner to register when the succession took place. It has been reported that for approximately 20% of private land in Japan it is already difficult to trace its actual owner. (Cf. Yoshihara (2017). See also Chap. 5 of this book).

owner, the government may use administrative subrogation (summary subrogation), but local ordinances cannot stipulate this measure.

1.2.2 National Legislative Measures

1.2.2.1 Unoccupied House Act

The Act on Special Measures for the Promotion of Countermeasures concerning Unoccupied Houses (hereafter, "Unoccupied House Act"), enacted in 2014 and fully put in force in May 2015, creates a standardized set of national protocols based on the measures already existing in local ordinances at municipal governments; further, it attempts to overcome the limitations of these aforementioned ordinances.

First, these measures attempt to identify the owners of unoccupied houses. Where referring to real estate registries alone does not identify the actual owner, the fixed asset tax division of a municipality may retain data on the owner based on its own independent investigations. However, the Local Tax Act barred the use of such tax information for purposes other than its original intended use. The Unoccupied House Act addresses this issue in Article 10 by pursuing the execution of the act and also allowing the legal use of the above personal tax information by municipal governments.

The second question is one of enforcement. Article 14 of the Unoccupied House Act stipulates that advice, guidance, recommendations, and orders can be executed against specific unoccupied houses.[14] This legislation serves to standardize the scope of measures for unoccupied houses. This article also stipulates the use of subrogation by the municipal government mayor where the owner of the property cannot be identified even after an investigation.

1.2.2.2 Amendments to the Local Tax Act

Around the same time as the enactment of the Unoccupied House Act, major amendments were made to special provisions concerning tax on residential fixed assets, one of the major causes of the growth in unoccupied houses. In a reform to the Local Tax Act in March 2015, shortly before the Unoccupied House Act was fully put in effect, new wording was added such that, where a "specific unoccupied house" is subject to a "recommendation" per Article 14, Clause 2 of the Unoccupied House Act, that plot of land can be excluded from special residential provisions. Furthermore, the Ministry of Internal Affairs and Communications, in a revised directive issued in May 2015 concerning the Local Tax Act, stated its opinion that, where a house is structurally deemed not to be a residence and is planned for demolishing or has not taken sufficient measures for residential use, "where the use of the house in question, or the state of its administration or other objective metrics find… that it is unlikely to

[14]The concept of "specific unoccupied houses" is to be described later.

be used for residential purposes in the future," it is exempted from coverage by the residential provisions aforementioned. As a result, even those dwellings that have not received a recommendation may be subject to a changing tax policy by the municipal government in question.

1.2.3 Features of Legislative Responses

What aspects can be seen in the legislative responses by the national government and by municipalities in addressing unoccupied houses as a problem of importance to society at large?

1.2.3.1 Framing as "Unoccupied House Problem"

Firstly, legislative responses to the various issues posed by unoccupied houses is not addressed within the framework of the Building Standards Act, which defines basic rules on all buildings, but rather through the creation of independent ordinances and special law (the Unoccupied House Act) which specifically focus on the issue of unoccupied houses. As described in Sect. 1.1, response to the unoccupied house problem has become a "social problem", so this phenomenon is indeed framed as the "unoccupied house problem."

The questions that therefore follow are, (1) is a given building defined as an unoccupied house and, if so, what is the definition of an unoccupied house?" and (2) if so, is the house in a state requiring legal intervention?

Definition of "Unoccupied Houses"

The Unoccupied House Act defines "unoccupied houses" at the "house or associated structure" level (Unoccupied House Act, Article 2, Clause 1). Therefore, according to interpretation by the Ministry of Land, Transport, Infrastructure, and Tourism, one of the ministries presiding over the act, "where only parts of row houses and certain shared residences are unoccupied…the house itself is not deemed unoccupied."[15] It adds that, "for housing complexes, even if most apartments or units do not currently contain residents, if there are any units with residents, the house as a whole is not considered unoccupied."[16] Many of Japan's apartments are forecast to have unoccupied units, making administration difficult. The Unoccupied House Act, however, does not address these vacant apartments. Municipal ordinances and the Unoccupied House Act specifically focus on unoccupied standalone residences.

---

[15]Ministry of Internal Affairs and Communications & Ministry of Land, Infrastructure, Transport and Tourism (2015b, p. 2).

[16]Miyaji et al. (2015, p. 57).

Secondly, municipal ordinances and the Unoccupied House Act define "unoccupied houses" as those which are "permanently unoccupied" (Tokorozawa Ordinance Article 2, Item 1) or "permanently in a state where they are not used for residential or other purposes" (Unoccupied House Act, Article 2, Para. 1). With respect to the notion of houses "permanently in a state where they are not used for residential or other purposes," policy by the Ministry of Internal Affairs and Communications and the Ministry of Land, Infrastructure, Transport, and Tourism[17] lists one standard as, "e.g., no particular record of usage of the house for roughly a year." Furthermore, the Ministry of Land, Infrastructure, Transport, and Tourism treats houses "used for storage" as "used for residential or other purposes".[18]

Indeed, given the provisions of the Unoccupied House Act, this legal interpretation seems logical. However, from the point of view of legislative policy, there is reason to question the treatment that "non-residential 'usage,' such as that for 'storage,' need not imply 'non-occupancy.'"

In the case of problems sustained by the neighboring area due to improper management of a residence, the interests of the house owner and the neighboring landowners or residents are at conflict. In this case, there is a substantive difference in houses in which a "resident" resides in them and those where he does not. For example, in cases where the resident owner stocks articles in the house—a so-called "trash house" that inconveniences neighboring residents—this would naturally not be considered "unoccupied", because she actually resides in it. Resolving the "trash house" problem requires multi-polar social support of the original resident; there is reasonable cause to distinguish these from the unoccupied house problem. A logical approach would be to categorize dwellings based on whether or not people are "residing" in them.

However, this may not necessarily apply to non-residential forms of "use." For example, a dwelling that is used for storage and does not qualify as "unoccupied" would, if excluded from the categorical scope of the law, make in-person surveys impossible. Instead, when considering what measures to take for dwellings deemed "unoccupied," the more sound legislative approach would be to compare and weigh the benefits the owner enjoys through use against the external burden placed on the environs and neighbors. Usage that would not be deemed suitable for economic or other reasons could potentially be interpreted as not meeting the Unoccupied House Act's definition of "use."[19]

---

[17]Ministry of Internal Affairs and Communications & Ministry of Land, Infra-structure, Transportation and Tourism (2015a).

[18]Ministry of Internal Affairs and Communications & Ministry of Land, Infrastructure, Transport and Tourism (2015b, p. 2).

[19]Ministry of Land, Infrastructure and Transportation also takes a position that only the management activity such as replacement of air will not constitute "use" of the housing. It also admits that a housing that has access "only about once in several years" will be regarded as "unoccupied" (Ministry of Internal Affairs and Communications & Ministry of Land, Infrastructure, Transport and Tourism (2015a, p. 2). See also Miyaji et al. (2015, pp. 50–56).

Focus on Negative Externalities in Environs

As described in 1.1, given that unoccupied houses in and of themselves are not necessarily the cause of this problem, the type of unoccupied houses that would be subject to legal measures would perforce be limited to a certain scope. Local municipal ordinances on unoccupied houses and the Unoccupied House Act focus on negative externalities in the neighboring environs and place restrictions like the following: An ordinance in Tokorozawa defines "houses in an unmanaged state" for the purposes above, as does the Unoccupied House Act's definition of "specific unoccupied houses."

"Specific unoccupied houses" as defined by Article 2, Clause 2 of the Unoccupied House Act is "(1) those in a state such that, if abandoned, would run the risk of collapse or other significant safety threat, (2) those in a state posing a significant threat to hygiene/sanitation, (3) those that, due to inappropriate management, significantly disturb the landscape, or (4) where, for the protection of the surrounding environs and environment, abandonment would be unsuitable. (Notation by this author)

Let us compare this to the previously-mentioned Tokorozawa ordinance. Article 2, Item 2 of the ordinance focuses on "an unmanaged state" and defines them as, "(A) Houses or other structures that, (i) due to age or typhoon or other natural damage, run the risk of collapse, or (ii) where the dispersion of building materials therefrom poses a risk or (B) those in a state where there is a risk of fire or crime caused by unauthorized entry by unspecified persons". (Notation by this author)

If we compare the definitions, the Unoccupied House Act's definition of, (1) "risk of collapse or other significant safety threat" is congruent with the definitions used in the Tokorozawa ordinance (and most other municipal ordinances). With respect to (2) "significant treat to hygiene/sanitation," the Tokorozawa Ordinance does not have a specific stipulation, but many local ordinances do stipulate something similar.

By contrast, while some local ordinances do define (3) "those that, due to inappropriate management, significantly disturb the scenic view" and (4) "where, for the protection of the surrounding environs and environment, abandonment would be unsuitable," they are comparatively few. In this way, the Unoccupied House Act is relatively unique in including these issues in its scope. However, while the Unoccupied House Act stipulates measures to order disposal of a house to remedy the issue of (1) and (2), it cannot issue orders for disposal with respect to (3) and (4).

Meanwhile, item B of the Tokorozawa ordinance (crime prevention measures) is not encompassed by the Unoccupied House Act.

In this way, taking legislative measures towards negative externalities to the neighborhood is tantamount to municipalities becoming involved in issues of neighborhood adjacency and pecuniary interests. Therefore, one could reasonably object by asking whether it is fair for neighboring residents or landowners to obtain pecuniary gain through the involvement of the government.

The presumed response is that in many cases, the location and name of the owner of an unoccupied house is unknown, so it is unrealistic for neighboring residents to be able to raise a civil suit against them, hence the assistance by the municipality is legitimized. However, difficulty in identifying the counterparty to a lawsuit is not limited to the unoccupied house problem.

Secondly, where there is harm to life or health, such as damage to public space like roads, and administrative involvement is presumed a matter of course, there could be a limitation of the scope of involvement. The wording of an "unmanaged state" as defined by the Tokorozawa ordinance seems to have been crafted with these limitations in mind. However, even where involvement was limited in cases of risk to life or health, caution is needed towards the fact that the involvement itself, insofar as it affects pecuniary interests, would be unchanged.

Further, the Unoccupied House Act's stipulation of "specific unoccupied houses" infringing on (3) (landscape) includes elements that would go beyond simple neighborhood externalities. The Ministry of Land, Infrastructure, Transport, and Tourism Guidelines[20] remark on the suitability of (3) that, "inadequate management of the property results in a failure to comply with rules on the existing landscape." Specifically, the determination for this is based on compliance with rules defined in the Landscape Act on landscape zones and plans. In this way, the Landscape Act's policies in this regard include elements pertaining to the public interest that are not resolved by the immediate issue of negative externalities to the neighborhood.

Further, there are other dimensions implicated in administrative involvement and individual interest in unoccupied houses. First, where the house owner and plot owner differ, measures taken for the house may affect the interests of both parties. Next, there may be cases where administrative procedures vis-a-vis the unoccupied residence are to the benefit of its owner rather than neighboring landowners. For example, where a residence is dismantled per subrogation, the owner must bear the costs of said procedure. If the owner is insolvent, collecting such fees is not realistically possible. Therefore, rather than voluntarily dismantling houses per advice and guidance, owners of unoccupied houses have a greater economic incentive to wait until they are subject to. We need to be aware of this moral hazard associated with execution of the Unoccupied House Act.

1.2.4 Use of the Unoccupied House Act

According to data compiled by the Ministry of Land, Infrastructure, Transport, and Tourism, current application of the Unoccupied House Act[21] amounts to 15,586 advice and guidance and 922 recommendations, 111 orders, and 41 administrative subrogations, as well as 124 executions by summary subrogation[22] (subrogation

[20] Ministry of Internal Affairs and Communications & Ministry of Land, Infrastructure, Transportation and Tourism (2015a).

[21] Ministry of Internal Affairs and Communications & Ministry of Land, Infrastructure, Transportation and Tourism (2019).

[22] Ministry of Internal Affairs and Communications & Ministry of Land, Infrastructure, Transportation and Tourism (2019, p. 2).

	FY2015	FY2016	FY2017	FY2018	Total
Advice and Guidance	2,890 (167)	3.515 (221)	4,271 (278)	4,910 (335)	15,586 (541)
Recommendation	57 (25)	210 (74)	285 (91)	370 (105)	922 (197)
Order	4 (3)	19 (17)	47 (30)	41 (19)	111 (56)
Administrative Subrogation	1 (1)	10 (10)	12 (12)	18 (14)	41 (34)
Summary Subrogation	8 (8)	27 (23)	40 (33)	49 (44)	124 (92)

*FY=fiscal year (Apr.~Mar.)

Fig. 1.4 Number of measures against specified unoccupied houses (the number in parentheses is the number of municipalities that took the measure). *Source* Ministry of Internal Affairs and Communications & Ministry of Land, Infrastructure, Transportation and Tourism (2019, p. 2)

where even a full survey fails to identify a specific owner[23]) since its enforcement in 2015 until March 2019 (Fig. 1.4). Compared to the traditional Japanese administrative approach of not exercising authority where possible, this is a comparatively high number.[24] In this way, the creation of the Unoccupied House Act has yielded some results.

1.3 Future Issues

1.3.1 Measures Beyond Disposal of Unoccupied Houses

To properly handle the unoccupied house problem, it is critical that measures beyond simply removing unoccupied houses are taken.

First, policies must be crafted towards the "utilization" of houses that are unoccupied. Where there is a special historical or scenic value to the houses or streetscape, they could be effectively utilized through renovation or conversion. For example, efforts are underway to utilize traditional dwellings as luxury hotels in Sasayama, Hyogo Prefecture, and the way in which traditional townhouses in Kyoto have been repurposed is another effective usage case. In terms of reusing unoccupied houses

[23] See Sect 2.1.

[24] Kitamura (2016, p. 48).

that do not have a "special" value, we can look to efforts to reuse housing projects and repurpose former central shopping arcades into multi-purpose zones.

Secondly, policies must be taken to foster distribution on the market. Unoccupied house "banks" and other projects where municipalities call for the registration of unoccupied houses and publish that information online in order to find buyers and renters are already underway. 603 municipalities that operate "unoccupied house banks" participate in integrated databases on national level operated by two private enterprises and supported by the Ministry of Internal Affairs and Communications and Ministry of Land, Infrastructure, Transport, and Tourism.[25]

Further, the Japan Trans-Housing Institute (JTI) operates a "My House Lease System"[26] in which JTI rents houses from their owners and leases them out to those seeking residences. Through this system, dwelling owners can provide rental housing to persons seeking domicile without interacting with them directly. In addition, a three-year fixed lease contract between the owner and JTI attempts to overcome the risk of the property not returning to the original owner after the resident's lease expires. However, the usage record of this legal scheme has been reported rather low.[27]

Thirdly, where dwellings age and are unfit for use, municipalities offer support for their scrapping and removal. Where using public funds to subsidize these projects, the question at issue is whether such public financing will enhance the public interest, not only individual private benefits. Where emergency measures require it, or where use of a demolished site is deemed public (including creating an open space for disaster responses, etc.), the usage would likely be justified.

1.3.2 Institutional and Theoretical Problems

The unoccupied house problem in some ways is representative of the contemporary phenomenon of underutilized land.[28] Japan's laws on use of land and cities have thus far been premised on the active use of land and were, therefore, focused primarily on curbing overuse, so they are not equipped to cope with issues posed by underuse. This suggests the need for a viewpoint focused not merely on unoccupied houses, but on shifting the structural basis of these laws themselves. Furthermore, the current understanding of property rights, which form the basis of land and urban laws, must be restructured to be more sensitive to externalities.[29]

As seen in 1.2, unoccupied houses are in and of themselves not an issue so much as these being a phenomenon indicative of problems in Japanese residential policy,

---

[25] https://www.mlit.go.jp/report/press/totikensangyo16_hh_000189.html. (Accessed 22 Mar 2020).

[26] https://www.jt-i.jp/lease/ (Accessed 22 Mar 2020). Cf. Akiyama (2016, pp. 162–165).

[27] According to H. Ohgaki, a director of the JTI, the usage record amounts to only 657 cases by Nov. 13, 2014. Asami et al. (2015, pp. 164–165).

[28] Cf. Takamura (2015).

[29] Yoshida (2016, p. 43).

the residential market, and urban planning. One of the most important points we will have to address in the future is creating a legal framework to effectively cope with the "sponge phenomenon" in urban areas in an era of shrinking cities.[30] The countermeasure against unoccupied house issue, is a typical indicator, which will demonstrate the efficacy of our legal system to deal with this issue of perforation.

Acknowledgements This work was supported by JSPS KAKENHI Grant Number JP26301008, JP15H03290, JP16H03681, and JP18KK0033.

References

Akiyama Y (2016) Akiya Mondai to Chintaishakuhō no Kadai (Unoccupied house problem and the task for the lease law). In: Yoshida K, Kadomatsu N (eds) Toshi Kūkan no Gabanansu to Hō (Law and governance of urban space). Shinzansha, Tokyo, pp 149–168

Asami Y et al (2015) Wākushoppu: Akiya Kaishō Katsuyō no Tame no Fudōsan Shisutemu ni Kansuru Gutaiteki Teigen ni Mukete (Toward a concrete proposal for the decrease and utilization of unoccupied houses). Nihon Fudōsan Gakkai Shi 28(4):161–171

Kitamura Y (2015) Shimpō Kaisetsu Akiyatō Taisaku no Suishin ni Kansuru Tokubetsu Sochihō (Commentary on the act on special measures for the promotion of measures for unoccupied houses). Hōgaku Kyōshitsu 419:55–64

Kitamura Y (2016) Akiya Hō no Jisshi ni okeru Hōteki Ronten(1) (Legal issues surrounding the implementation of unoccupied house act (1)). Jichi Kenkyū 92(10):47–61

Kobayashi H (2016) Jinkō Genshō Jidai no Machidukuri (Town-building in the age of population decline). Jumin Gyōsei no Mado 435:4–13(9)

Ministry of Internal Affairs and Communications (2019) 2018 Housing and land survey (Jūtaku Tochi Tōkei Chōsa). https://www.stat.go.jp/data/jyutaku/index.html. Accessed 22 Mar 2020

Ministry of Internal Affairs and Communications & Ministry of Land, Infrastructure, Transportation and Tourism (26 Feb 2015a) Akiyatō ni Kansuru Shisaku wo Sōgoteki Katsu Keikakuteki ni Jisshisuru Tame no Kihonteki na Shishin (Basic guideline for comprehensive and well planned enforcement of measures regarding unoccupied houses). http://www.mlit.go.jp/report/press/house03_hh_000097.html. Accessed 22 Mar 2020

Ministry of Internal Affairs and Communications & Ministry of Land, Infrastructure, Transportation and Tourism (26 May 2015b) Result of the public comment procedure regarding the draft guideline for the measures againstspecified unoccupied Houses. http://www.search.e-gov.go.jp/servlet/PcmFileDownload?seqNo=0000129798. Accessed 22 Mar 2020

Ministry of Internal Affairs and Communications & Ministry of Land, Infrastructure, Transportation and Tourism (31 Mar 2019) Akiyato Taisaku no Suishin ni Kansuru Tokubetsu Sochihō no Sekōjōkyotō ni tsuite (On the actual situation of enforcement of the Unoccupied Houses Act). https://www.mlit.go.jp/common/001297115.pdf. Accessed 22 Mar 2020

Ministry of Land, Infrastructure, Transportation and Tourism (2013) Sankō Shiryō: Chūko Jūtaku Ryūtsū Sokushin ni Kansuru Kenkyūkai (Reference material: research group on facilitating distribution and utilization of used residences). http://www.mlit.go.jp/common/001002572.pdf. Accessed 22 Mar 2020

Ministry of Land, Infrastructure, Transportation and Tourism (21 Apr 2015a) Material No.7 for the 36th meeting of panel on infrastructure development, subcommittee on housing and land. http://www.mlit.go.jp/common/001087737.pdf. Accessed 22 Mar 2020

[30]Cf. Ministry of Land, Infrastructure, Transport and Tourism (2017).

Ministry of Land, Infrastructure, Transportation and Tourism (26 May 2015b) Result of the public comment procedure regarding the draft guideline for the measures against specified unoccupied Houses. https://search.e-gov.go.jp/servlet/PcmFileDownload?seqNo=0000129798. Accessed 22 Mar 2020

Ministry of Land, Infrastructure, Transport and Tourism (2017) Toshi no Suponji ka e no Taiō (Measures Against "Sponge Phenomenon" in Cities) https://www.mlit.go.jp/common/001197384.pdf. Accessed 22 Mar 2020

Ministry of Land, Infrastructure, Transportation and Tourism (2019) Heisei 30 Nendo Jūtaku Chakkō Tōkei ni yoru Saikenchiku Jōkyo no Gaiyō (Overview of the Situation of Reconstruction based upon the Survey of Housing Construction 2018). https://www.mlit.go.jp/statistics/content/001314503.pdf. Accessed 22 Mar 2020

Miyaji K, Nishimura A, Yamashita T (2015) Akiya Taisaku Tokubetsu Sochi Hō no Kaisetsu (Commentary on the act on special measures for the promotion of measures for unoccupied houses). Taisei Shuppansha, Tokyo

National Institute of Population and Social Security Research (2017) Population Projections for Japan (2017): 2016 to 2065. http://www.ipss.go.jp/pp-zenkoku/e/zenkoku_e2017/pp_zenkoku2017e.asp. Accessed 22 Mar 2020

Nozawa C (2016) Oiru Ie Kuzureru Machi (Aging houses, collapsing towns). Kodansha, Tokyo

Spector M, Kitsuse JI (2017) (first published 1987). Constructing social problems. Routledge, New York

Takamura G (2015) Kashō Riyō Jidai ni okeru Shoyūkenron Saikō (Reflections on the Right to Property in the Age of Underuse). Hōshakaigaku 81:64–75

Yoshida K (2016), Akiya Mondai wa Tochi Shoyūken ni Donoyona Eikyō wo Ataeru ka (What impact does the unoccupied house issue have on land property?). Geppo Shihoshoshi 534:36–45

Yoshihara S (2017) Jinkō Genshō Jidai no Tochi Mondai (Land problem in the age of population decrease). Chuō Kōronsha, Tokyo

Chapter 2
Municipal Responses to Vacant Properties in the United States

Abstract This chapter will examine how municipal code enforcement departments, along with other governmental actors at various levels, respond to vacant residential property problems in the U.S. The first part of the chapter will provide a general account of the causes and effects of the vacant house crisis in the U.S. The second part of the chapter will focus on municipal responses. After a brief overview of the different geographical levels of government in the U.S. system, the chapter will explain the inadequacies of traditional building code enforcement tools in preventing and abating vacant property nuisances and sets out what tools municipal governments need in order to respond effectively to the problem of vacant houses.

Keywords Vacant house problems · Indiana's unsafe building law · Foreclosure · Baltimore's vacant building receivership ordinance · Land banking

2.1 Introduction

In the United States, the majority of older, industrial cities struggle with vacant house problems. At the extreme, Detroit and Flint, both automobile manufacturing centers in Michigan, have residential vacancy rates of more than 15%. Baltimore, with a little more than 7% of its houses vacant, has the third highest rate of vacancy of any U.S. city. Far from being evenly distributed across the entire city, these derelict, vacant houses are concentrated in the poorer communities. Detroit's most severely distressed neighborhoods have approximately 40% of their houses in an unoccupied, derelict condition. While property abandonment at this intensity dominates life in these communities, the affects and costs are felt across the nation.

Because the vacant property crisis in the U.S. is a national matter, every level of government has a role to play in confronting it. Yet, cities, as the lowest level of government in the U.S., bear the primary responsibility for the health and safety of besieged neighborhood residents. This chapter will examine how municipal code enforcement departments, along with other governmental actors at various levels, respond to vacant residential property problems in the U.S. The first part of the chapter will provide a general account of the causes and effects of the vacant house

N. Kadomatsu et al., *Legal Responses to Vacant Houses*,
Kobe University Social Science Research Series,
https://doi.org/10.1007/978-981-15-6641-7_2

crisis in the U.S. The second part of the chapter will focus on municipal responses. After a brief overview of the different geographical levels of government in the U.S. system, I will explain the inadequacies of traditional building code enforcement tools in preventing and abating vacant property nuisances and set out what tools municipal governments need in order to respond effectively to the problem of vacant houses.

2.2 Causes

As detailed below in the discussion of their neighborhood effects, derelict vacant structures are highly visible burdens on the communities in which they are located. Yet vacant houses and lots are better understood as a result of rather than a major cause of the decline of American industrial cities. Housing prices are invariably driven by the attractiveness of life in that community. The tremendous gap in demand for inner-city and suburban land has little to do with proximity to particular natural geographic features, but is largely determined by the quality of local public goods such as schools, public safety, and shopping and recreational amenities.[1] Many inner-city neighborhoods have high concentrations of poverty, a reality that strongly shapes education, crime, and commerce in those places. The 20th-century middle-class exodus from central cities to the surrounding suburbs was clearly driven by the rise of the automobile, but other forces have shaped the severe economic segregation that characterizes many U.S. metropolitan areas.

The foundation for small independent municipalities, or suburbs, on the fringe of larger cities was laid by early-20th-century legislative action to prohibit cities from annexing new residential developments being built on their boundaries.[2] Free from being compelled to join their urban neighbors as city taxpayers, the suburban residents could form their own local governments and provide their own roads, emergency services and schools. Developers of suburban housing tracts, with the encouragement of lenders and banking regulators, sold to homebuyers of European descent ("white") and required racially restrictive covenants that prevented resale to non-whites.[3] While the practice continued for some time after the U.S. Supreme Court declared them unenforceable in its 1948 decision of *Shelley v. Kraemer*,[4] the main mode of exclusion thereafter shifted from explicitly racial segregation to one that focused on class.

Through exclusionary zoning, suburbs prevented the construction of dense single-family and multiple-family housing that would have facilitated socioeconomic integration.[5] Even as the courts moved to integrate schools racially, suburban districts

[1]Fischel (2001, pp. 45–46).

[2]Tyson (2012, pp. 303–23).

[3]Massey and Denton (1993, pp. 51–55).

[4]334 U.S. 1 (1948).

[5]Fischel (2001, pp. 65–71).

were exempted from judicial orders requiring transfer of students across jurisdictional lines unless those suburbs had a history of deliberate racial discrimination.[6] Since these suburbs had little or no history at all, their land was not affected by the taint of a racist past. The message to the middle class was clear: A family with the economic ability to choose its neighborhood should move to the land of the fresh start, the suburbs.[7]

In the inner city, the loss of the manufacturing jobs that first induced migration from the rural areas to the cities led to severe unemployment, civil unrest, and epidemics of violent crime, drug abuse, and chronic disease.[8] Baltimore's 1950 population of almost 950,000 shrank to a 2010 low just beneath 621,000, a decline of 35%. Even as the overall metropolitan area grew, Baltimore's population dropped by double-digit percentages in both the 1970s and 1990s. A city built for a million residents came to have more than 30,000 vacant houses and vacant lots. As with many under-crowded urban communities, neither the population loss nor the housing vacancies are equally distributed throughout the city.

The much smaller city of South Bend, Indiana also experienced about a 30% loss in population from 1970—six years after its primary industrial employer, Studebaker, closed for good—to 2010.[9] A handful of neighborhoods on the west side of town lost more than half their populations during those four decades.[10] The majority of the more than 1,000 vacant and abandoned properties in South Bend are located in these largely African-American and poor neighborhoods,[11] but other South Bend neighborhoods also have derelict, vacant houses.[12] While these less distressed neighborhoods, not just in South Bend but in many other cities as well, suffer the full range of urban problems that tamp down demand for housing in the inner city, their higher housing values keep vacant house renovation economically possible.

2.3 Effects

While the mortgage crisis also impacted housing projects not yet completed, nearly vacant houses were occupied, with their last occupants frequently being renters, defaulting borrowers or elderly homeowners. Both technically and generally, the term "vacant" differs from "unoccupied" by degree of time. "Vacant" is often defined as unoccupied for more than 90 days. In and of itself, a house's lack of occupancy, even over a lengthy period of time, does not violate any valid criminal statute or housing regulation. Yet long-term vacancy is often accompanied by neglect and

[6] Milliken v. Bradley, 418 U.S. 717, 782 (1974).
[7] Milliken v. Bradley, 418 U.S. 717, 801 (1974).
[8] Wilson (1987, pp. 20–92); Hanlon (2010, pp. 69–70).
[9] Vacant and Abandoned Properties Task Force Report (2013, p. 7).
[10] Vacant and Abandoned Properties Task Force Report (2013, p. 8).
[11] Vacant and Abandoned Properties Task Force Report (2013, p. 10).
[12] Vacant and Abandoned Properties Task Force Report (2013, p. 10).

decay. The elements—water, sun, and acute changes in humidity and temperature—subject roofs, windows, siding, gutters, and, eventually, interior components to endless assault. With lack of use comes loss of rent, dwindling of vigilance, and deferral of maintenance. The decline of the house exterior makes the deterioration apparent to all who see it.

Vacant houses are also targets of more deliberate forms of destruction and misuse. In little or no time, mischief makers can cause a degree of damage to a building that nature would take years to inflict. Scavengers seeking valuable scrap metal will rip the copper plumbing and wiring right out of the walls. Such careless destruction can lead to floods or even gas leaks that endanger nearby homes and their occupants. In 2010, fifteen families on Cleveland's west-side were left homeless by a gas explosion in a vacant house ransacked by a thief stealing copper and appliances.

Once compromised–by human activity, weather, or the combination of the two—derelict properties remain open to any who care to enter, at least until they are properly secured. Whether or not they are boarded up, the neighborhood is harmed. Houses open to casual entry encourage trespassing and more serious criminal activity. A survey of unsecured vacant houses found 83% of them evidenced unlawful occupancy and/or illegal use.[13] These wood-frame houses are all too often exposed to cooking or warming fires. The resulting calls for emergency assistance force police, fire, and medical first responders to enter dark and treacherous interiors.

Even if it is not a serious danger, an unoccupied house in need of repair may be noted and seen as a sign of neighborhood decline. A boarded-up property rarely escapes notice and leaves a strong impression of deterioration. In a classic article on neighborhood change, James Wilson and George Kelling demonstrated how small, seemingly superficial signs of disorder can accelerate decline. The central relevance of vacant houses to their account was evidenced by the piece's title: *Broken Windows*.[14] People who have options as to where they might live are unlikely to purchase a home on a block with a boarded-up house on it. They may not even want to live on that block as a tenant. Nevertheless, cities may wish to encourage owners of vacant properties to secure them despite their increased visibility. Closed-up buildings are preferable to houses that are open to casual entry. Not surprisingly, some municipalities, such as Augusta, Georgia, has enacted local laws that set out a permit process for "mothballing" vacant houses.

Whether boarded or unsecured, a visibly uninhabitable vacant house imposes significant costs on neighbors, the surrounding community, and the local government. These properties promote crime, harbor vermin, and put children at risk. Neighboring homes face the prospect of fire and water damage. An adjacent owner may struggle to obtain affordable fire and liability insurance because of the condition of the house next door.[15] A study by U.S. Federal Reserve Bank economists showed that each derelict

[13] Spelman (1993, pp. 481- - 95).
[14] Wilson and Kelling (1982, p. 29).
[15] Vacant Properties (2005, p. 11).

vacant house diminishes the market value of occupied houses within a two-block radius by at least 1.3% per vacant house.[16]

2.4 Vacant Property Response Objectives and Constraints on Achieving Them

The government's ability to respond to and prevent vacant property problems is rooted in its authority to abate, mitigate and prevent nuisances. A nuisance is an activity or set of conditions that threatens health and safety or interferes with the property rights of another. The states and their local subdivisions have broad authority to regulate private property to prevent, mitigate and abate nuisances. The police power of governments in the United States, including a local government properly authorized by its state legislature, is not limited to just nuisance activity; it extends to the public welfare more broadly. Yet regulations that go beyond protecting the public interest in eliminating nuisances must contend with powerful protections for private property under the U.S. Constitution. Under the 5th and 14th Amendments, governmental interventions that go "too far" in interfering with the investment-backed expectations of private property owners will be struck down as invalid in the absence of compensation even if they are not otherwise outside the legitimate scope of the government's authority to regulate in matters of health, safety and welfare.[17] Laws that directly address nuisance situations, however, do not risk being overturned as regulatory takings.[18] The courts have consistently held that no property owner has the right to maintain a nuisance. Thus, any regulation limiting or prohibiting a nuisance cannot be an infringement upon core private property rights.

Even the most aggressive governmental action, if carefully tailored to eliminate a nuisance, will neither be invalidated under the Due Process Clause nor found to give rise to a compensation claim under the Takings Clause. Certain remedies, however, such as demolition, appointment of a receiver, or even direct remedial action on a property by a government agency, may not be justified if the property in question is not a nuisance.[19] Moreover, even if the overall condition of the property justifies demolition or some direct intervention to carry out repairs, mandated work to correct violations unrelated to the nuisance may be challenged as unconstitutional and/or lacking legal authority.[20]

Even if the legislature does extend to local governments the legal authority to engage in aggressive nuisance abatement to new circumstances, takings jurisprudence complicates the legislature's ability to limit a property owner's compensation

---

[16]Whitaker and Fitzpatrick (2012, p. 2).

[17]Pennsylvania Coal Co. v. Mahon, 260 U.S. 393 (1922).

[18]Mugler v. Kansas, 123 U.S. 623 (1887).

[19]Ypsilanti Charter Tp. v. Kircher, 761 N.W.2d 761, 778 (Mich. App. 2008).

[20]Ypsilanti Charter Tp. v. Kircher, 761 N.W.2d 761, 778 (Mich. App. 2008).

claim for deprivation of property rights. While the U.S. Supreme Court has continuously held that true nuisance abatement can never be the basis for a takings claim, it has also held that a government action that results in a total deprivation of value can be justified only by nuisance in its historical sense.[21] By focusing on the limits of private property being shaped by "the background principles of nuisance," the majority opinion in Lucas v. South Carolina Coastal Council seemed to halt a legislature's ability to create new categories of nuisance, at least in the context of total takings. Yet if the common law and the legislature were to come to different conclusions as to what risks, of the same type, were so imminent as to constitute a nuisance, it is not at all clear that a court hearing a takings claim could disregard the statutory line. Thus, while the legislature could not extend this defense to a total takings claim to types of property problems that had not traditionally been regarded as nuisances, it can apparently deem certain familiar risks to be a nuisance even if courts had previously ruled that the danger or bother posed to the public was too remote to be rise to the level of a nuisance.

The capacity of municipal governments to respond to and to prevent vacant property nuisances requires them to be able to bring about physical changes to and to compel transfer of ownership of delinquent properties. Cities bear the responsibility for code enforcement, but legal reforms are needed. Before introducing the argument for municipal empowerment and relating the specifics of the reforms, it is necessary to give a little background about the levels of government in the United States.

When comparing the different federal, state, county and municipal levels of government, it is important to remember that each level has its own executive and legislative branches, which are, in general, directly elected. Counties and cities are legal subdivisions of their states, but their political leadership is locally elected not appointed by the statewide government. States are the basic units of the U.S. governmental system. As such, fundamental issues of private law are determined by the states, not by the federal government and not by the local units. In the event of conflict, federal law takes precedence over state law, but the federal government is allowed to legislate only on subjects that go beyond matters internal to a particular state's boundaries. While the regulation of banks that are nationally chartered is an important, relevant area of federal law, the most significant power of the federal government is its ability to tax across the entire nation. The federal government provides money for most urban community development activity.

Municipalities are creations of the state government. They have only the powers that the states give them, but all states have chosen to give cities the ability to enforce health and safety measures with regard to residential property. As such they can set building code standards and provide for administrative fines for violation and, in some cases, a range of administrative and perhaps even judicial remedies.

Basic traditional code enforcement methods do not work as well with vacant buildings as they do with occupied rental properties. Fines can motivate repairs better in the case of occupied properties because repairs are usually more manageable and

---

[21] Lucas v. S.C. Coastal Council, 505 U.S. 1003 (1992).

landlord wants to keep the rent coming. At $50 per square foot, a modest total rehabilitation of a 1500 ft^2 vacant house would cost $75,000. Even houses that can be made ready for occupancy for substantially less nearly always require more than the $10,000 that the average demolition and removal would cost. Since elimination of a vacant house nuisance always involves a major capital investment, no sensible response strategy can ignore the importance of the return on that investment. Even if an owner is willing to make repair expenditures that cannot be recaptured through increased use, income or resale value, no lender may be willing to provide the necessary funds. With so much money involved, the financial advisability of rehabilitation often dictates whether or not it goes forward.

No factor will limit the return on rehabilitation investment more than the weakness of the neighborhood real estate market. If the best homes on a block are not selling for more than $50,000, investing $75,000 in a full-scale rehabilitation of a vacant property on that block is not financially prudent. For many older, inner-city neighborhoods in South Bend and similar cities, houses without major defects can be purchased for less than $25,000.[22] Once these properties have fallen into disrepair, however, the market will not support their renovation. Traditional code enforcement does not render such considerations irrelevant. In a marginal case, the inducement of fines and, possibly, imprisonment may well motivate an owner to rehabilitate a property that would otherwise languish.[23] Yet in situations where the verdict of the market is unequivocal, renovation is unlikely, even with governmental coercion.[24]

When major capital investments are required to achieve basic compliance with the law, then traditional enforcement standards and mechanisms may not be effective. Just as major environmental cleanups cannot be achieved by resort to laws against littering, the abatement of vacant house nuisances, by rehabilitation or demolition, cannot be achieved by building code standards designed for the construction and upkeep of occupied houses. The most commonly used construction code in the United States, the International Building Code, makes some provision for unsafe vacant buildings. Cities truly plagued by vacant properties have had to amend the code to specify standards and remedies that meet their enforcement needs. As a code that focuses on the upkeep of existing structures rather than overseeing the permit process for new construction, the International Property Maintenance Code, first promulgated in 1998, has been a common starting point for these communities. Other cities have looked to the state government to create an entirely separate law empowering them to deal with vacant properties in a comprehensive manner.

Section 116 of the International Building Code (IBC) provides for the definition of and official response to unsafe structures. The law provides the local building official with the authority to identify structures as unsafe and ensure that they are "taken down and removed or made safe."[25] Unsafe buildings include those that are "insanitary, deficient in light and ventilation or adequate exit facilities, constitute a

---

[22]Kemp (2001, p. 310).

[23]Kemp (2001, p. 215).

[24]Kemp (2001, p. 215).

[25]Int'l Bldg. Code Section 116.1 (2012).

fire hazard or are otherwise dangerous to human life."[26] Apart from declaring any vacant structure that is "not secured against entry" to be unsafe,[27] the IBC does not explicitly address vacant buildings as unsafe structures. It does not delineate what kinds of structural deficiencies are unsafe when a building has no one living, or even going, inside it regularly. Baltimore has amended its version of the International Building Code to clarify when the City is empowered to cite the owner of a vacant property and when it may take action, including repair or demolition, directly. As discussed below, it has also used its Building Code to create a unique receivership remedy. Yet to get a sense of how vacant building code standards and remedies differ from those for occupied properties, we first need to look at Indiana's Unsafe Building Law.

2.5 Indiana's Unsafe Building Law

Rather than try to amend its version of the IBC, South Bend, Indianapolis and other affected cities persuaded the state legislature to adopt an Unsafe Building Law (UBL). As defined by the UBL, an unsafe building includes any building, whether commercial or residential, whether occupied or vacant, that is a fire or public health hazard, a public nuisance, or subject to a structural impairment or serious code violation.[28] Additionally it includes any vacant or blighted building that is unfit for human habitation.[29] A debris-free, secure, unoccupied house is not subject to the Unsafe Building Law unless it is not fit to be lived in. A securely boarded, vacant house; however, is subject to the UBL because a house with boarded windows is not habitable. More importantly, being subject to the Unsafe Building Law does not mean being subject to every remedy available under the UBL. The statute requires that any remedy used be an appropriate response to the harm caused by the property. Thus, a boarded-up house could not be demolished just because it was boarded up.

The UBL authorizes several different types of administrative orders that can be issued by the local code enforcement agency directly, without prior approval from a judge. The orders can require any or all of the following that are reasonable given the condition and type of property:

- That a building be vacated immediately
- That a building be sealed up against entry
- That pest control be performed
- That debris and trash be removed

---

[26] Int'l Bldg. Code Section 116.1 (2012).

[27] Int'l Bldg. Code Section 116.1 (2012).

[28] Ind. Code. Section 36-7-9-4 (2017).

[29] Ind. Code. Section 36-7-9-4 (2017).

- That a building be rehabilitated in compliance with the IBC
- That a building be partially or completely demolished, if warranted
- That a building be sealed and maintained to look like nearby buildings.[30]

There is no violation under the UBL until the deadline in an issued order has come and gone without compliance. The deadline must normally be between 10 and 60 days from the issuance of the order, and the time given for compliance must be sufficient for the mandated action to be completed.

Notice of the order must be provided to any and all owners of the property. If the order calls for demolition, then mortgagees must also receive notice. Orders that require vacating, demolishing or special sealing and maintenance of a building must provide for a hearing date so that the order can be reviewed by an independent hearing officer.[31] All other orders must inform the owners that they have 10 days to request a hearing or the order will become final.[32] At any hearing on the order, the independent hearing officer may affirm the order, modify the order or rescind it altogether.[33]

When an order has not been complied with by the deadline, the code enforcement authority may take any of the following actions:

- Issue civil penalties for lack of compliance 60 days past the deadline
- Request hearing officer to issue civil penalties for willful refusal to comply
- Take direct action to carry out the order
- File a court action (can be filed by a community organization also):
  - to order the owner(s) to comply
  - to issue civil penalties
  - to appoint a receiver that may rehabilitate and/or sell the property
  - to authorize the petitioner to carry out the ordered action.[34]

For all the variety of legal tools and procedural avenues offered by the UBL, true abatement of an abandoned house nuisance is achieved in one of only two ways: the house is rehabilitated, or the house is demolished. As alluded to earlier, which solution a code enforcement official pursues depends on the economic feasibility of rehabilitating the property, which is determined by how the cost of the repairs needed compares to the surrounding property values. If a neighborhood market is already distressed, very few significant property repairs will be cost-effective. Yet the question remains: why should the economic feasibility of rehabilitation determine whether or not rehabilitation is pursued as a goal by a code enforcement official enforcing the law (especially when demolitions are invariably funded by taxpayers)?

An owner's ability to see a reasonable return on rehabilitation investment determines whether or not the renovation happens primarily because most owners do not have sufficient disposable cash to fully fund the needed repairs themselves. If they do

[30] Ind. Code. Section 36-7-9-5 (2017).

[31] Ind. Code. Section 36-7-9-4 (2017).

[32] Ind. Code. Section 36-7-9-5 (2017).

[33] Ind. Code. Section 36-7-9-7(d) (2017).

[34] Ind. Code. Section 36-7-9-10, 17-20 (2017).

not, then they will need to borrow money to carry out the repairs. Any bank lending on the property will want to know that the resulting resale value of the property will be high enough to secure repayment of the loan. If the neighborhood market is too weak, no one will voluntarily invest in the renovation.

While an owner with deep pockets may be cajoled into making a financially detrimental renovation investment, threats of liens against the property will not make for effectively incentivize remedial action as the owner has already accepted the fact that he or she will not be seeing any further income from the property. Nor should code enforcement officials assume that it will be easy to convince a hearing officer or a judge that an owner with the cash to fix up an abandoned house in a distressed neighborhood should be punished with fines or jail for his or her refusal to renovate. If there are other vacant houses that are not being rehabilitated, such an owner may be allowed to pay for demolition or nuisance mitigation instead.

Even though it makes sense that the lack of economic return may rule out renovation, it still may not be clear why a code enforcement official should pursue rehabilitation of a property instead of demolition just because the neighborhood is still strong enough to reward renovation investment. When such a neighborhood has any abandoned houses, it is already moving closer to the point where it no longer has the market strength to encourage significant capital investment. Clearly a vacant lot is preferable to an abandoned house, but a renovated house speaks to the neighborhood's strength far more effectively than does a public demolition of the derelict structure. If the choice was between receiving some relief through immediate demolition and waiting indefinitely for a possible renovation, the neighbors most affected by the abandoned house would almost certainly prefer the vacant lot as a new neighbor. To really keep marginal neighborhoods viable, however, code enforcement officials have to develop tools that can achieve rehabilitation quickly even when the owner is unable to see the job done.

The first thing to note about the UBL approach to repair orders is that they are not merely orders to make the property safe. Since the UBL takes pains to make clear that not every noncompliant, unoccupied house meets the statutory definition of an unsafe building, one might easily think that an order to repair is merely an instruction to the owner to put the property back into a condition that does not qualify as "unsafe" under the statute. Yet that would be wrong. Once a house has become unsafe as defined by the UBL, code enforcement officials are authorized to order the owner to make the property fully compliant with the Indiana Building Code, assuming that is the standard applied by the local government. If it were otherwise, code enforcement officials would be playing a rather pointless cat-and-mouse game in which owners of vacant properties that slipped into a derelict condition could make code enforcement go away with a few belated superficial repairs. As it is, UBL allows code enforcement officials to order owners of abandoned houses to get them ready for occupancy.

In some cases, the mere issuance of an order to the owner of an abandoned house can spur an owner to action, especially if the code enforcement official has been careful to restrict such orders to economically feasible rehabilitations. Yet fines and/or court orders will be necessary for other owners. The imposition of fines can be an important way for a local government to recoup revenue from its enforcement efforts, but fines, or even the threat of them, can make an owner move forward on a renovation that previously had been delayed indefinitely. For other, more defiant, owners, only confrontation by a judge will be enough to get them to do what the law requires. When an administrative hearing officer finds that an owner has willfully refused to comply with a rehabilitation order, the most he or she can do is impose civil penalties. A judge, on the other hand, can find an owner who willfully disobeys a court order in contempt of court. Fines for contempt can be large and mount on a daily basis. Arrest and incarceration are also remedies available to a court committed to seeing an owner comply with an order.

The Unsafe Building Law authorizes non-emergency demolitions of privately owned structures based on confirmation at an administrative hearing. The UBL requires that a hearing be held even if no one requests one or even makes any response to the notice of demolition order. The UBL also mandates that mortgagees and anyone else with a substantial property interest in the abandoned house be sent notice of the order and the hearing. This requirement means that any local government that wishes to order a property demolished in a non-emergency situation must do a title search on the property before sending out notice of the demolition order and hearing. Moreover, if a respondent contests the order and loses, any appeal taken will result in a full rehearing of the case in court, but such an appeal must be filed within 10 days of the hearing officer's decision. If an order to demolish a property is upheld at the hearing and, at the time, no appeal is pending and the deadline for compliance has passed, then code enforcement officials may, upon further notice to the owners and mortgagees, arrange to have the abandoned house demolished, with the owner liable for the costs.

As noted earlier, the fact that an abandoned house meets the definition of "unsafe" does not necessarily mean the order to demolish it will be upheld. In reviewing demolition orders the courts have held the fact that a building may yet be repaired could be a reason to rescind a demolition order. Yet they also have consistently found that when it appears that it is not likely that an owner actually will rehabilitate a property, then a demolition order will be affirmed. As frustrating as delays caused by owners claiming to be on the verge of making repairs may be, the true constraint on demolitions in communities with many abandoned houses is lack of funds. Cities have turned to Community Development Block Grant (CDBG), then to successive iterations of the Neighborhood Stabilization Fund (NSF) program and most recently to the Hardest Hit Fund. Nevertheless, the need exceeds the available resources.

Demolition should not be the response to a property that can be rehabilitated without resort to public subsidy. Having a vacant lot next door can be a welcome relief to households that have had to live next door to a derelict, vacant houses for months if not years. Yet neighborhoods that currently have sufficient strength in their housing markets to incentivize investment in vacant houses need to preserve and build on that strength. Vacant lots mark a community as one in decline. Even if enforcement measures that bring about rehabilitation take longer than those that achieve demolition, the long-term benefits of having an occupied property rather an empty space can be critical in the struggle to preserve the strength of the neighborhood. Sometimes demolition becomes the preferred mode of abatement not because the house is too badly damaged for an economically feasible renovation but because the owner is unwilling or unable to make the repairs. In such cases, the tools for code enforcement must be able to force the transfer of a property to an owner that can bring about the economically feasible rehabilitation of the vacant property.

2.6 The Importance of Being Able to "Fire" the Owner

A strategy to obtain repairs by forcing a recalcitrant owner to internalize the costs that the vacant property is inflicting on the community makes sense when that owner is a rational actor with the ability to remedy the situation. Yet sometimes the owner, even when coerced by fines and threat of imprisonment for contempt of court, will not accede to pressure. More commonly the owner lacks the resources to carry out the renovation. Even if the owner, however, is able both to recognize and move forward on a plan to return the property to productive use, he or she may not be in a financial position to reap the benefits of any investment in the property. In these cases, the property is subject to excessive mortgage or other secured debt to give any hope to the owner of clearing a profit on it.

On occasion, an owner may lack the executive functioning necessary to carry out the rehabilitation even when it is both financially feasible and rewarding. Overseeing the renovation of an old house can be very demanding. Some property owners will not be up to the challenge. In some cases, the owner's propensity for mismanagement or serious personal vulnerability may have contributed to the property's decline. When lack of capacity is clear, certain enforcement measures may not be available. A court will not use fines or threats of imprisonment to coerce those owners who are truly unable to comply.[35]

The power of court to punish a defendant owner for failure to obey an order to abate a nuisance may seem the perfect remedy for an owner who intentionally evades his or her responsibility under the law with the hope of more easily making a profit. Such an owner may have the resources to make all the necessary repairs to a single derelict but instead chooses to buy many such properties in otherwise stable neighborhoods. By speculating on rising land values without investing in renovations, the investor may see a greater return by evading his or her responsibility to the surrounding community on whose efforts to improve the neighborhood his or her scheme depends. Aggressive enforcement may force the speculator into compliance but only if the attorneys prosecuting the action can succeed in having the owner personally served with notice of the proceedings. The high level of notice and opportunity to be heard applied in injunction and judicial contempt cases may prove particularly favorable to investors who hide behind out-of-state business entities or live great distances from their investments.

An owner unwilling or unable to make repairs not only makes compliance by rehabilitation unlikely but also limits hope that a voluntary transfer to a rational,

[35] Kinning (1993, p. 181).

capable owner will happen. An owner unable to fix the property may also turn down reasonable purchase offers due to a completely unrealistic view of its worth. Such an owner may have a strong personal attachment to the property even though it is no longer habitable. The speculator, assuming he or she can even be contacted, may be willing to sell for a reasonable price but also may be inclined to wait for higher appreciation.

Even when an owner is willing to transfer the property, a sale of the property may not be feasible because of claims on it by creditors. Owners of properties that wish to borrow money can pledge their properties as collateral. Owners who owe money may find their property likewise subjected to creditor liens. Whether voluntarily or involuntarily created, a lien against a property gives a creditor a priority claim against the value of that property. A lien creditor may have a statutory right to force the liquidation of the property in order to get repayment, but even if no such foreclosure action is feasible, the lien will survive voluntary sale from one owner to another.

A vacant property subject to multiple liens may place the parcel beyond the market's reach due to the transaction costs involved in resolving the vying claims on it. Anyone buying the property will want to acquire only once it is free and clear of any liens and encumbrances. If the owner is in default, the mortgagee may have the legal right to foreclose but elect not to pursue foreclosure because of doubts about the property condition and the strength of the neighborhood real estate market. Without the foreclosure, the owner has legal title but no financial stake, while the lender has a financial interest but lacks legal title. When a bargain-and-sale transfer is unavailable, a title-clearing mechanism such as a super-priority lien foreclosure may be the only feasible response. In all the cases described above, foreclosure on a super-priority lien presents an attractive alternative to court-ordered coercion. By forcing such owners to realize that ignoring their responsibilities will cost them their ownership of the property, a foreclosure based on failure to comply with code takes a new approach to cost internalization, one in which the cost imposed on the responsible party is liquidation of their ownership interest.

An owner who is forced to choose between eliminating the nuisance or having his property sold to those who are willing to fix it faces the true market judgment regarding the decision to invest in rehabilitation. If the property is not worth fixing up right away, there will be no foreclosure because there will be no buyers willing to take on the responsibility of rehabilitating the property. If, however, the property is located in a neighborhood strong enough to support investment in it, then the stakeholders are put to the question as to whether they will preserve their interests and carry out the renovation or step aside and take the cash value of their stakes in the property in its current condition.

Foreclosure produces better cost internalization than traditional code enforcement in certain cases for two reasons. First, the in rem approach to procedural due process is not as burdensome as for civil and criminal contempt proceedings and does not lead to a battle of wills with intransigent defendants.[36] Second, the cost being shifted onto the

[36] Kelly and James (2004, pp. 217–18).

noncompliant owner in foreclosure is no longer a fine of questionable collectability but the imminent loss of his or her ownership in the property.[37]

2.7 Baltimore's Vacant Building Receivership Ordinance

To be able to "fire" the owner for failure to abate nuisance conditions on his or her property, a municipality needs a lien foreclosure process with three characteristics. First, the lien must be created by the city's claim for costs associated with its code enforcement actions, including repairs the governments to stabilize the property. Second, the lien must take precedence over all private liens on the property. Third, the foreclosure auction in which the property is sold must be limited to bidders who have already demonstrated their willingness and ability to renovate the property immediately upon purchase.

Since 1990, Baltimore, Maryland has had a process that meets all three of these criteria. Its version of the forerunner to the International Building Code[38] provides the City with the power to file a lawsuit requesting that a judge appoint a receiver for the derelict.[39] In order to avoid the appointment of the receiver, an owner, a mortgagee, or any other party with a preexisting interest in that property has to present a plan to rehabilitate the property and post a bond to guarantee completion.[40] If appointed, the receiver's expenses, administrative as well as remedial, become a super-priority lien on the vacant property.[41]

Vacant building receivership law in other jurisdictions are modeled on analogous statutes for occupied apartment buildings and require long waiting periods prior to a receiver's foreclosure on his or her special lien. Baltimore's ordinance, however, authorizes the court to have the receiver foreclose on this lien before rehabilitation work has even begun and auction the property off to any bidder who has demonstrated the ability to rehabilitate the property immediately.[42] At its core, this remedy imposes a super-priority lien for failure to eliminate a vacant building nuisance. The fact that the receiver's lien takes priority over all preexisting private mortgages and liens allows the threat of foreclosure to be effective against lenders as well as owners. If these parties do not step forward to fix the property, then the receiver is able to offer a clean title to those who will.[43]

Baltimore's approach is somewhat unique in that it authorizes the court to order the sale of the property before the code violations have been corrected.[44] The transfer

[37] Johnson (2008, p. 1194).
[38] Bldg., Fire, and Related Codes of Balt. City, Int'l Bldg. Code Section 121 (2013).
[39] Bldg., Fire, and Related Codes of Balt. City, Int'l Bldg. Code Section 121.2 (2013).
[40] Bldg., Fire, and Related Codes of Balt. City, Int'l Bldg. Code Section 121.7 (2013).
[41] Bldg., Fire, and Related Codes of Balt. City, Int'l Bldg. Code Section 121.13 (2013).
[42] Bldg., Fire, and Related Codes of Balt. City, Int'l Bldg. Code Section 121.10 (2013).
[43] Bldg., Fire, and Related Codes of Balt. City, Int'l Bldg. Code Section 121.9 (2013).
[44] Bldg., Fire, and Related Codes of Balt. City, Int'l Bldg. Code Section 121.10 (2013).

itself to a qualified bidder is part of the remedial strategy.[45] By allowing a pre-screened buyer to purchase the property in its dilapidated state, this approach allows the party that is going to ready the property for productive use to handle the entire rehabilitation process.[46] Other receivership statutes require the receiver to eliminate the outstanding code violations as a prerequisite to any foreclosure on the unpaid lien.[47] If the property is to be sold in anything less than pristine condition, it is of great importance that bidders at the auction be pre-qualified as developers willing and able to rehabilitate the property. Transferring the property from one delinquent owner to another does nothing to remedy a vacant house nuisance. Many cities have broad authority to conduct urgently needed repairs to the exteriors of vacant houses and impose super-priority liens without judicial appointment of a receiver.[48] When foreclosed these liens enter into the general tax sale process in which an array of speculators and debt collectors bid alongside experienced developers.[49] For a receivership sale remedy to be an effective and legitimate means of achieving code compliance, the process of screening bidders for a receivership sale must ensure that the properties will be renovated promptly.

2.8 Tax Foreclosure and Land Banking

If a vacant house is located in a market that is too weak to support the investment needed to bring the property into compliance, a foreclosure based on failure to adhere to code standards is not an appropriate response.[50] Neighborhoods with multiple vacant properties require the kind of investment coordination that only land banks can provide. These governmental authorities can facilitate neighborhood revitalization by acquiring all the derelict properties in a neighborhood and make them available to developers who will rehabilitate them contemporaneously. Property tax foreclosure provides the most common acquisition method for land banks. The weakness of the real estate markets in these neighborhoods facilitates tax foreclosure by discouraging owners from paying property taxes on the vacant houses and lots they own.[51]

Every state provides some statutory scheme for collecting unpaid property taxes by foreclosure. The vast majority of states use a combined sale and foreclosure process to ensure both that the taxes due are paid in full and that any leftover value in the property is made available to the stakeholders whose interests have been liquidated. Most mortgage foreclosure proceedings auction the property only after

---

[45] Kelly and James (2004, p. 219).

[46] Kelly and James (2004, p. 219).

[47] Ohio Rev. Code Ann. Section 3767.41(I)(1) (West 2013); R.I. Gen. Laws Section 34-44-12 (West 2013).

[48] Mallach (2010, p. 47).

[49] Mallach (2010, p. 47).

[50] Kelly and James (2004, p. 226).

[51] Kelly and James (2004, p. 211).

the borrower's time to redeem has elapsed. In property tax collections, however, most proceedings to foreclose the equity of redemption occurs only after the property tax lien has been sold to a private bidder.[52]

Some states grant tailored periods of redemption for different types of property interests. Although Kansas is patient with homestead owners, giving them three years to pay, owners of vacant buildings receive only one year after the sale to prevent foreclosure.[53] Kansas has decided that the community should not have to be particularly patient with owners of unoccupied properties when "there has been a failure to perform reasonable maintenance."[54]

Crucial to the success of tax sale foreclosure as both a collection remedy and a means of clearing title to abandoned properties is the super-priority nature of the property tax lien, which allows it to take precedence over not only ownership interest but also mortgage and judgment lien interests the predate the tax delinquency[55] Because claims for unpaid property taxes take priority over pre-existing private liens, all parties with substantial interests in the property are entitled to notice of their opportunity to redeem. Constructive notice, such as publication of an advertisement in a newspaper of general circulation, can constitute constitutionally adequate notice, but only after diligent attempts at direct notification have been made.[56]

Effective reform of tax foreclosure laws impacting vacant properties requires attention to the procedures for the sale of liens as well as to the time for redemption afforded the owners and other stakeholders. A sensible approach to the sale of tax liens on vacant and abandoned houses and the lots resulting from their demolition allows local jurisdictions to facilitate investment coordination without fear of severely underpricing important receivables. A similarly tailored approach to the waiting period between the sale of a tax certificate on a vacant and abandoned property and the issuance of a deed for that property recognizes the urgency of getting such a property back into productive use without undercutting the rights of other owners, especially homeowners, to raise the money needed to prevent loss of their land to foreclosure.

Unoccupied, derelict properties located in neighborhoods with insufficient market strength to support their rehabilitation require special tax sale procedures to facilitate their return to productive use. A great many of these properties could not be sold, after a complete renovation, on the open market for just the costs of the needed repairs. That is, even if one such vacant house could be transferred in its dilapidated condition to a new, capable owner for $1, the needed renovations would still not be economically feasible. As discussed above, allowing a developer or team of developers to invest in all the vacant houses in a neighborhood offers a way to reset the market paradigm that has previously constrained the influx of desperately needed capital. The prevalence of significant tax delinquency makes tax foreclosure an ideal way to allow coordinated

---

[52] 26 U.S.C. Section 6323 (2013).

[53] Kan. Stat. Ann. Section 79-2401(a) (2) (West, Westlaw through 2013 Reg. and Special Sess).

[54] an. Stat. Ann. Section 79-2401a(a) (2) (West, Westlaw through 2013 Reg. and Special Sess).

[55] Alexander (2000, p. 760).

[56] Mennonite Bd. of Missions v. Adams, 462 U.S. 791, 798 (1983).

title-clearing efforts. Unfortunately, the great size of tax arrearages, when combined with legislated tax sale rules that require a minimum bid no less than the amount of the tax delinquency, prevents these properties from even taking the first step toward reconnection with the market.[57]

While minimum bid provisions may make sense for tax sales generally, they significantly harm efforts to return tax-delinquent vacant properties to productive use. Many, if not all, states require that any bid at a conventional tax lien auction to purchase a tax-delinquent property be sufficient to pay the relevant state and local government taxes and related charges due on the property.[58] Generally, the potential for corruption and abuse in a mass auction of public receivables justifies the legislature's insistence on receiving the full value of what the public is owed. Vacant and abandoned properties with large tax arrearages invariably remain unsold at the end of tax sales with such minimum bid requirements.[59]

Land banking efforts, however, are demonstrating that vacant and abandoned properties can be transferred to developers capable of returning them to productive use as long as an auction mechanism is not relied upon either to identify those buyers or to set the price of the sale. To accomplish the appropriate bundling and pricing of vacant properties in need on investment coordination, land banks must be empowered to purchase and foreclose on vacant property tax certificates without being required to pay the full lien value. As publicly accountable entities, they need to be able to work with potential developers to identify coordinated investment opportunities and sell the properties at prices that reflect the market realities and the public benefit of having the properties returned to productive use. Auctions do not allow for the verification of capacity and financing required for large-scale redevelopment projects nor do they allow for the negotiations needed to produce thoughtful pricing of the real property assets. To facilitate an ultimately more efficient mode of vacant property disposition, minimum bid requirements must be abandoned to allow transfers of qualifying tax certificates to land banks. States, such as Kansas, have recognized the need to set post-tax-sale redemption periods at different lengths to protect different kinds of property ownership. Those states facing significant concentrations of vacant properties in their urban neighborhoods must shorten the minimum time for completion of the foreclosure. For instance, Maryland requires most tax-sale purchasers to wait six months before commencing judicial foreclosure proceedings, but properties that have been certified as in need of substantial repair can be foreclosed upon after 60 days.[60] The waiting period is eliminated altogether for tax sale certificates sold at special bulk sales designed to facilitate land banking efforts.[61] Likewise, Indiana requires a delinquent owner to redeem a property within one year of a conventional tax sale;[62] Yet, it shortens that redemption period to 120 days for properties sold at

---

[57] Alexander (2011, p. 30).

[58] Alexander (2011, p. 30).

[59] Alexander (2011, p. 30).

[60] Md. Code. Ann. Section 14-833 (a), (e) (2013).

[61] Md. Code. Ann. Section 14-833 (f) (2013).

[62] Ind. Code. Section 6-1.1-25-4 (a) (1) (2010).

a special sale without the standard minimum bid requirement.[63] These clear and reasonable differences in redemption periods follow from the fact that foreclosure of vacant properties, by definition, do not result in the displacement of legal occupants. Moreover, the community need for investment in these properties requires a quicker transition than that allowed to tax-foreclosed properties generally.

To properly address the problem of house abandonment in their cities, municipal officials must have conventional code enforcement standards and procedures adapted to the context of vacant properties. Ultimately, this evolution of code enforcement strategy involves being able to force an owner to carry out an economically feasible rehabilitation or lose his or her property through a special foreclosure process. For those neighborhoods that lack the market strength to incentivize rehabilitation with public subsidy, a form of land assembly using tax foreclosure is needed. As explained above, each of these require legal reforms that are being enacted in various places within the United States.

References

Alexander Frank S (2000) Tax liens, tax sales and due process. Indiana Law J 75:747–808

Alexander Frank S (2011) Land banks and land banking. Center for Community Progress, Washington

Fischel William (2001) The homevoter hypothesis. Harvard University Press, Cambridge

Hanlon B et al (2010) Cities and suburbs: new metropolitan realities in the U.S. Oxford, Routledge

Johnson Creola (2008) Fight blight: cities sue to hold lenders responsible for the rise in foreclosures and abandoned properties. Utah Law Rev 2008:1169–1254

Kelly Jr, James J (2004) Refreshing the heart of the city: vacant building receivership as a tool for neighborhood revitalization and community empowerment. J Afford Hous Commun Dev Law 21:210–238

Kemp Robert L (2001) The inner city: a handbook for renewal. McFarland Publishing, Jefferson

Kinning Robin Powers (1993) Selective housing code enforcement and low-income housing policy: Minneapolis case study. Fordham Urban Law J 21:159–198

Mallach A (2010) Bringing buildings back: from abandoned properties to community assets, 2nd ed. National Housing Institute, Montclair

Massey Douglas S, Denton Nancy A (1993) American apartheid: segregation and the making of the underclass. Harvard University Press, Cambridge

Properties Vacant (2005) The true cost to communities. Center for Community Progress, Washington

Spelman William (1993) Abandoned buildings: magnets for crime. J Crim Justice 21:481–495

Tyson Christopher J (2012) Localism and involuntary annexation: reconsidering approaches to new regionalism. Tulane Law Rev 87:297–352

Vacant and Abandoned Properties Task Force Report (2013) https://southbendin.gov/wp-content/uploads/2018/05/Code_FinalVATF_Report_2_red.pdf. Accessed 21 Mar 2020

Whitaker S, Fitzpatrick IV, Thomas J (2012) The impact of vacant, tax-delinquent and foreclosed property on sales prices of neighboring homes. https://www.clevelandfed.org/en/newsroom-and-events/publications/working-papers/2011-working-papers/wp-1123-the-impact-of-vacant-tax-delinquent-and-foreclosed-property-neighboring-homes.aspx. Accessed 21 Mar 2020

Wilson JQ, Kelling GL (1982) Broken windows. Atl Mon, 29–38

Wilson William Julius (1987) The truly disadvantaged. The University of Chicago Press, Chicago

[63] Ind. Code. Section 6-1.1-25-4 (c) (2010).

Chapter 3
Expropriation of Vacant Property in France: The Case of Substandard Housing

Abstract Expropriation practices in the context of urban renewal projects offer an interesting vantage point from which to view the local management of abandoned housing. This chapter describes the general issue of vacant properties in France, referring to data available on scope and location. It briefly reviews the legal and political positions on policy instruments to combat vacant housing in France, from *incentive* (public subsidies for housing improvement) to *directive* tools (requisition, expropriation). Lastly, the chapter focuses on an empirical study examining expropriation of substandard housing in the Paris region.

Keywords Vacant property · Expropriation · Requisition · Substandard housing · Litigation

3.1 Introduction

Vacant properties and substandard housing are not equivalent notions: vacant homes are not all unsafe and substandard housing is often occupied before the implementation of expropriation. But expropriation of substandard housing frequently involves vacant properties, often linked to the tricky legal question of compensation. For that reason, an empirical inquiry into expropriation practices in the context of urban renewal projects offers an interesting vantage point from which to view the local management of abandoned housing.

Expropriation is not per se a procedure for addressing vacancy issues in France. No special provision relates to the implementation of expropriation for the acquisition of vacant properties. Theoretically, the absence of explicit regulations is not in itself a legal barrier to the use of expropriation in that case. Since the 1958 Ordinance issued during the De Gaulle Presidency, "public utility" (the legal basis for expropriation) has become a general notion: it does not refer to particular kinds of development. However, the use of expropriation for the sole purpose of acquiring isolated vacant properties would be legally weak by case law standards. Usually, public utility projects involving vacant properties come under a wider objective, like urban regeneration of the neighborhood or production of social housing.

N. Kadomatsu et al., *Legal Responses to Vacant Houses*, Kobe University Social Science Research Series, https://doi.org/10.1007/978-981-15-6641-7_3

One reason why expropriation is commonly used to address vacancy issues is the difficulty of implementing the other legal tools *explicitly* directed at vacant properties. In French law, while instruments like *requisition of vacant housing* have long (since the second world war) been part of the legal toolkit for planning policies, their long-term implementation is hampered by lack of political support.

3.2 Vacant Properties in France: General Context in Urban and Rural Areas

In France, the main regions with a tradition of vacant property are economically and demographically declining areas (ANAH 2014; Bessière 2003). These regions are predominantly rural and seldom previously industrialized. High vacancy rates are observed outside of urban and suburban areas.

It is important to point out that there are *no large shrinking cities* in the French housing market. Significant vacancy rates (between 10 and 20%) are observed in several French cities, but these are *medium-sized* cities (under 100,000 inhabitants) *located in rural regions.* Analysis of *vacancy rates* and data on the *number of vacant homes in absolute terms* yield very different, almost "reverse", results. Data on vacancy rates inform us about the frequency of vacancy at the local level: on average, rural and remote municipalities more frequently contain vacant homes than urban municipalities. But urban spaces contain most of the vacant housing *in absolute terms*, even though in relative terms vacant homes represent a tiny proportion of total housing. This is clearly exemplified by the Paris region, where the large quantities of vacant homes only account for a tiny part of total housing.

However, while vacant property remains an issue only in medium-sized cities, it has increased dramatically during the last decade (ANAH 2014). The post-2008 economic crisis widened the gap between dynamic regions (large conurbations, coastal areas) and declining areas. A particularly important factor in the increase of vacant property was the major cuts to public subsidies for housing improvement during the period.

Several reports on the French housing market reveal that combatting vacancy rates is an effective housing strategy, but only to a limited extent (Robert and Coloos 1992). It cannot be considered the main strategy for tackling the housing crisis: building new dwellings is still viewed in France as the principal remedy for the housing shortage. Assessment of the number of vacant properties is controversial: the data available from the tax administration do not adequately represent the scale of the problem. But most studies point out that only a minority of vacant properties are actually suitable for immediate residential use. Different reasons are given: the vacancy may be temporary (the owner intends to sell), the cost of renovations may be higher than producing new housing, demand for housing may be too low in an economically depressed area, etc. (Fabre and Nicol 1979). However at local level, dealing with vacancy rates is still a significant challenge for planning policies. In urban areas, reducing vacant homes is important to revive the local economy. In rural and periurban areas, furthermore, reutilizing vacant housing is part of a planning strategy against urban sprawl. Lastly, the significant stock of vacant homes in large conurbations remains an opportunity for housing development.

3.3 Legal and Political Debates on the Instruments for Reducing Vacant Housing

The housing policies aimed at combatting housing vacancy in France consist of three components: tax policies, public subsidies for renovation and prescriptive tools inducing public control of private properties.

3.3.1 Incentive Policies on Vacant Homes: Tax and Subsidies

A tax on vacant properties was introduced specifically to deter property owners from leaving dwellings unoccupied (Act of July 19, 1998), and was reinforced in subsequent years. However, the tax rate remains low, apparently too low to have a significant impact on the behavior of owners (Conseil d'État 2009). Furthermore, owners can easily avoid the tax by placing an advertisement in a rental agency, without actually renting their property.

The proceeds from this tax are used to finance a public agency (Agence nationale d'amélioration de l'habitat, ANAH, "national housing improvement agency"). This agency provides financial assistance to owners unable to meet renovation costs and helps them put their real estate back on the housing market. As mentioned above, the large budget cuts during the last decade significantly impacted the agency, reducing the number of vacant homes put back on the market.

3.3.2 Directive Instruments Depriving Owners of Property Rights: Requisition and Expropriation

French legislation provides for different legal instruments to infringe private property for reasons of public interest: pre-emption, expropriation and requisition (Struillou 1996). We will focus on the two last instruments, those most commonly used to address the vacancy issue.

Requisition of private properties was first established in public law during the 1930s to grant the State significant prerogatives in case of war (Law of July 11, 1938). But after the Second World War, requisition evolved into a legal instrument for housing policies outside the war context (Ordinance of October 11, 1945, under article L. 641-1 of the Building and Housing Code). In the post-war period, France experienced a severe housing shortage due to destruction from the war, increasing rural exodus, and a demographic boom. The precarious living conditions of homeless or poorly housed people, and the informal extension of slum areas in the Parisian suburbs, were major areas of concern. According to the 1945 Ordinance, the Prefect (head of the State administration at local level), is entitled to requisition "vacant, unoccupied or insufficiently occupied housing" if so requested by the municipal council. The requisitioned housing is allocated for a five-year period to destitute persons (for example, people expelled from housing). In addition to the Prefect, the mayor is also empowered to order requisition, but in more limited contexts (where there is obvious danger to the neighborhood) (article L. 2212-1 of the Local Authorities Code).

The requisition law remained largely unchanged until, in the late 1990s, the socialist government incorporated new provisions under a comprehensive reform aimed at combatting poverty and social exclusion (Act of July 19, 1998, under article L. 642-1 of the Building and Housing Code) (the act that established a tax on vacant properties). The new provisions identify (through numerical standards) municipalities where housing needs are critical. In these municipalities, owners (both individuals and corporate entities) of requisitioned properties are required to sign a lease agreement with the municipality (or other local public bodies). The public body then allocates the housing to a needy person, on a rather long lease of up to 12 years.

The numerical impact of requisition proved disappointing, for three main reasons. The first reason is that, as mentioned above, the number of immediately available vacant properties is limited. The second is that other tools are usually preferred by local authorities (friendly agreements, or expropriation). The third reason is absence of continuity in different government approaches. After the 1998 Act, the Housing Ministry gave detailed instructions to the State services to initiate a systematic survey of vacant housing that might be subject to requisition. But subsequent governments abandoned this survey. More recently, there has been a renewal of interest in requisition procedures: the Access to Housing Act (Act of March 24, 2014) empowered local public bodies to decide on requisition without a Prefect's order. However lack of political support for requisition of vacant homes has been the long-term picture over the last decades.

In an official report on housing policies, the State Council (the French supreme administrative court) pointed out how few properties were actually requisitioned, even in a period of strong political support (about 400 dwellings for the year 2001 in the Paris region, for example) (Conseil d'État 2009). The numerical impact of the procedure is difficult to evaluate, however, as the mere threat of requisition is likely to help the public authorities to obtain friendly agreement with the owner (to rent or sell the vacant property to private persons or to public bodies). Furthermore, as requisition does not induce any transfer of property (unlike expropriation), it appears financially attractive for public authorities (there are no acquisition costs) (Théron 2005). For that reason, there continues to be academic and political debate over government intervention via requisitions.

As explained above, the management of vacant properties also involves expropriation procedures. Unlike requisitions, however, they are not generally linked specifically to vacancy issues. Vacant housing is expropriated in the context of development operations linked to larger goals (creation of social housing or renovation of unsafe or substandard housing) and concerning more properties than a single vacant dwelling. As previously mentioned, the expropriation of a single property for the purpose of acquiring a vacant home would be legally weak by case law standards (judicial review verifying that "infringement of private ownership shall not be excessive").

The French parliament has sought to authorize public utility orders (the legal basis for expropriation) on the sole grounds of acquiring vacant homes. In 2009, Parliament debated a law proposing to "combat vacant housing" by entitling municipal councils to urge the Prefect to issue a public utility order concerning housing vacant "for an excessive period" (more than 5 years) (Draft Bill of November 10, 2009, French Senate). But the draft bill was finally rejected by the Senate on the grounds that the reform proposed would be too detrimental to private ownership. The practical consequence of this aborted reform is that expropriation of vacant property, while easier to justify in the context of substandard housing, remains difficult to implement for high-value properties that are kept unoccupied for purposes of speculation.

3.4 Disputes Over Compensation for Expropriated Properties and the Vacant Housing Issue: Empirical Data from Civil Courts

In a socio-legal perspective, I examined 174 expropriation cases collected from local civil courts in the Paris region during a three-year period (2007–2009). An extended analysis of this inquiry was presented in a previous publication (Melot 2013). In this study, I propose to focus on the issue of vacant properties from the angle of expropriations concerning substandard housing in this sample. From disputes over compensation, we obtain a much more complex picture of the situation than that of the court simply recording expropriating authorities' offers.

3.4.1 Expropriation in the French Legal System

In French law, properties coming under a public utility order can be expropriated. The beneficiaries are usually local authorities, but the right to decide on public utility is a prerogative of the State (the decision is taken by the central government for large projects and by the Prefect for local developments). The public utility order can be contested by concerned parties (owners as well as local residents or associations) by filing a claim with an administrative tribunal (Hostiou et al. 2015).

Once expropriation is granted, the owners also have the alternatives of either negotiating a settlement or filing a claim against the purchase price offered by the developer. In that case, the expropriations judge (from a local civil court) drafts the court order officially transferring the property. This judge also intervenes to set just compensation, that is to say, the purchase price on which the interested parties could not reach agreement. During the procedure, an expert assessor from the tax administration (land tenure department) issues an independent advisory opinion on the claims in the dispute, which the judge is free to follow or reject. According to administrative data on expropriations for public utility, around 10% lead to dispute. While expropriation is only rarely implemented, the very existence of this possibility, always underlying negotiations, is a determining factor in the vast majority of cases of acquisition by mutual consent.

3.4.2 Compensation Disputes and Strategies of Vacant Property Owners

Owners of substandard dwellings run the risk of illegal occupation by squatters. Residential buildings declared unsafe by the local administration and likely to be expropriated in the short term tend to become abandoned (Dietrich-Ragon 2011). This leaves their owners in a strategic dilemma over whether to deploy valuation strategies (ensuring the housing is vacant to obtain higher compensation, which any existing tenant's rights would diminish) that may increase the risk of illegal occupation.

Expropriation cases reveal that owners go for a third group of strategies, for example rent-free agreements safeguarding both their properties and their compensation awards. Another kind of dispute concerns the valuation of apparently vacant properties that owners claim to be occupying as their own residence. According to the law, housing situated in unsafe buildings must be renovated or destroyed. For this reason, the properties must be valued with reference to the land value, not to the housing market. This method of evaluation particularly penalizes expropriated owners, with the sole exception of owners that have occupied the dwelling for a long time as a personal residence.

Therefore, the legal strategy of many owners consists in proving they make personal residential use of the expropriated housing. In a case in the Batignolles district of Paris, the judge conducted a site visit of several vacant dwellings belonging to the same owner in a dilapidated building. The judge states in his report that *"all the dwellings are run down, except one that apparently has just been renovated… Windows have been replaced and a new floor has been installed. After a few questions, the owner admitted that the renovation is recent. But in spite of this rehabilitation, the housing remains dilapidated" (Paris Expropriation Court, March 12, 2007, case n 06–00264)*. Establishing whether there is actual residential use is thus a divisive issue between parties to the proceedings (municipalities accusing expropriated owners of implementing recent rehabilitations to create an illusion of private residential use).

3.4.3 The Value of Vacant Properties: How to Evaluate Compensation When There Is No Longer a Market?

In regeneration areas with a lot of vacant dwellings, complex issues of property valuation are raised by expropriation cases. The usual methods of valuation through comparison of market transactions at the local level cannot be implemented. The local real estate market does not work normally, and should be considered as a "closed market".

When disputes over compensation of expropriated owners occur, it has long been common for the only buyer at the local level to be the public agency in charge of the regeneration program. The consequence of the property valuation problems in declining neighborhoods can be observed empirically from a statistical analysis of disputes: expropriating authorities and judges more often fail to converge on property values for substandard housing than in other cases (Fig. 3.1). In a collapsed market, expropriating authorities are required to simulate the normal functioning of a "free" real estate market. They refer to transactions either from the past or related to distant areas when estimating the current value of properties in shrinking neighborhoods.

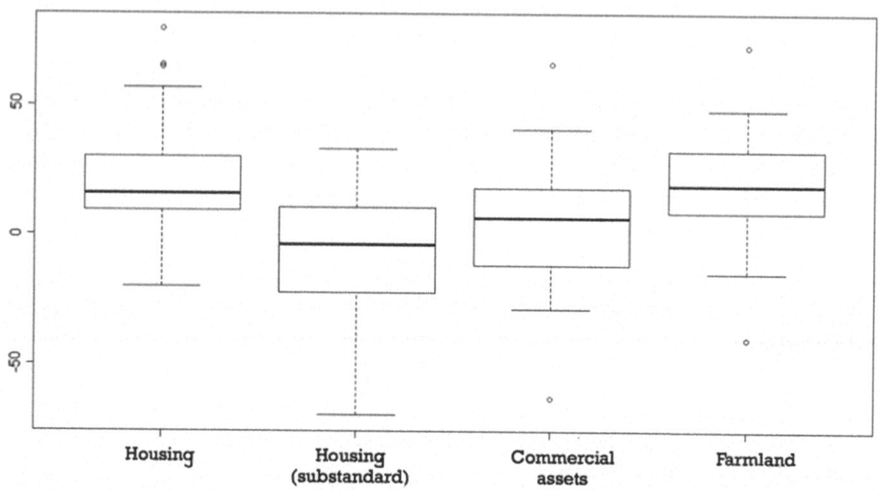

Fig. 3.1 Diverging evaluations (in %) of property value between expropriating authorities and civil courts. *Source* (Melot 2013), from cases collected from civil courts in the Paris region (n = 154). Comment: The scatter plots graphically represent the dispersion of values. The bold lines inside the plot represent the median value, the lines outside the box are the upper and lower quartiles. The longer the box, the more dispersed the values. Diverging evaluations are observed most frequently where substandard housing is involved

For example, in a case from a poor neighborhood in a northern suburb of Paris (city of Montfermeil), the assessor from the land tenure department points out that the evaluation made by the public developer is controversial *"as for the past five years there has no longer been any free market in the area" (Bobigny Expropriation Court, December 19, 2007, case n 59–07)*. The simulations by the expropriating authority are thus based on theoretical fictions, and the questionable criteria applied are often contested by those expropriated and even by the judges themselves.

Another indication of the difficulty of property valuation in this context is that expropriating authorities predominantly refer to judicial precedents by default when setting the value of the expropriated assets, because the declining market does not provide sufficient transaction references. But judges are sometimes reluctant to validate this kind of "default" evaluation. In a judgment by the civil court of Paris concerning vacant buildings in a renovated neighborhood, the expropriation judge considered that the evaluation proposed by the public body was particularly weak, as *"it refers principally to former judicial decisions, which are not based on references to recent market values" (Paris Expropriation Court, March 26, 2007, n°06–00307).*

3.5 Conclusion

Legal strategies for expropriation cannot be satisfactorily explained without taking into account judicial practices at a local level. In the context of substandard housing, the strategies observed in expropriation cases relating to vacant properties highlight the ability of the expropriated parties to construct legal fictions aimed at valuing their compensation rights under optimum conditions. Such claims force judges to choose between conflicting objectives: is it the right to full compensation that should come first? Or should priority be given to combatting housing speculation? Through the apparently limited perspective of civil cases involving disputes over compensation, we can identify general issues in the relations between owners of vacant properties and public bodies pursuing urban renewal.

References

Agence nationale de l'amélioration de l'habitat (ANAH) (2014) Memento de l'habitat privé. http://www.anah.fr/fileadmin/anah/Mediatheque/Publications/Les_chiffres_cles/anah_Memento_2014.pdf. Accessed 15 Dec 2016

Bessière S (2003) La proportion de logements vacants la plus faible depuis trente ans. INSEE Première, n 880, janvier

Conseil d'État (2009) Droit au logement, droit du logement. Rapport public. La Documentation française, Paris, 459 p

Dietrich-Ragon P (2011) Le logement intolérable. Presses Universitaires de France, Paris

Fabre F, Nicol C (1979) Les logements vacants ne sont pas tous disponibles. Economie et statistiques, n 107, janvier

Hostiou R, Struillou J-F, Melot R (2015) Expropriation in France. In: Sluysmans J, Verbist S, Waring E (eds) Expropriation Law in Europe. Nijmegen (The Netherlands), pp 157–176

Melot R (2013) La valeur en procès: expropriation et stratégies judiciaires. Editions Adef, Paris

Robert C, Coloos B (1992). Rapport sur le fonctionnement du marché du logement et de la vacance (Paris, Lyon, Marseille), Ministère de l'équipement et du logement

Struillou J-F (1996) Protection de la propriété privée immobilière et prérogatives de puissance publique. L'Harmattan, Paris

Théron S (2005) La réquisition administrative de logement, Actualité de jurisprudence de droit administratif, p 247

Chapter 4
The Urban Planning Development Concept as a Central Instrument for Managing Apartment Vacancies in German Law

Abstract In some regions of Germany, the phenomenon of shrinking cities can be observed. Urban planning development concepts are focusing on urban redevelopment to manage these shrink processes. These concepts bridge the gap between urban planning legislation and individual decisions and are designed for problem and are designed to define and solve problems/define problems and implement solutions. They are made obligatory by administrative agreement between the federal government and the federal states, depend on urban construction funding programmes of the federal government and the European Union, and are embedded into legal regulations geared toward cooperative and consensual administrative action.

Keywords Shrinking cities · Urban governance · Sustainable city development · Urban planning development concept · Informal planning

4.1 Introduction

Shrinking cities are a German, a European and a global phenomenon. Despite a concurrent growth of many cities, there is a decrease in population in many places as well.[1] This leads to major consequences for a city's infrastructure in terms of urban planning. Sustainable city development appears to be especially at risk, as these developments prevent an economically worthwhile focus of public resources, unnecessarily seal areas that are not needed from an ecological perspective, and render social integration into an urban community uncertain. Addressing such problems differs paradigmatically from the guiding principles underlying urban planning legislation in the past, which were geared toward growth. This contribution examines the development concept as regards urban planning, a central institute of construction law, which has been created within German law to handle these processes of change. It is characterized by the fact that urban construction law seeks to carry out the

[1]Cf. contributions in: Richardson and Nam (2014).

*Assistant Professor Dr. Arne Pilniok
Hamburg, Germany
arne.pilniok@uni-hamburg.de.

N. Kadomatsu et al., *Legal Responses to Vacant Houses*,
Kobe University Social Science Research Series,
https://doi.org/10.1007/978-981-15-6641-7_4

defining and solving of problems cooperatively. At the same time, urban construction law needs to maintain the equilibrium between the structural safeguarding of public interest and taking the logic of action of the affected public and private actors into account. Therefore, an initial look at the actual findings is required (2.). Subsequently, the normative foundations of the urban planning development concept shall be assessed (3.). This is only to be understood in the context of its regulatory structures, especially those of the federal government's urban development funding (4.).

4.2 Actual Findings in Germany

The initial step is to gauge the regionally limited decline in population in Germany and its causes (2.1). Subsequently, the consequences of shrinking cities will be considered, being particularly relevant to the legal responses (2.2).

4.2.1 Shrinking Cities and Their Causes

In recent decades, shrinking cities may be observed primarily in most of the East German municipalities with the exception of some larger cities, and partially in West German federal states as well, namely in the Ruhr area. The causes of these shrink processes are difficult to isolate. Rather, they are complex interrelations that have to be considered according to their regional differences. For the German development, three interconnected trends comprise the main focus—even though they may be generalized to a certain extent. Firstly, a decrease in population in these areas is occurring, which can, however, not be traced back to a decline in the birth rate as the population in total in Germany is, also due to migration from outside the EU, is steady.[2] But there are, in fact, different processes of internal migration, in addition to demographic change. These are closely connected to the fact that, secondly, there is an underlying regular structural change within shrinking processes, which correlates with problems for the regional job market and, thus, pushes outflow processes from the East to the West and from rural areas to the cities. This issue goes far beyond a deindustrialization. Thirdly, migration away from urban areas may be observed, in part, as a result of the structure of the housing market.[3] Despite a change in legal tax conditions, the preferences are still largely geared toward the acquisition of vacant individual properties. The demand for such houses cannot be satisfied in

[2] Kühn, M. & Liebmann, H. (2009). Regenerierung schrumpfender Städte—eine Einführung. In Kühn and Liebmann (2009, p. 14) et seq.

[3] Ibid., Kühn and Liebmann (Eds.) (2009, p. 15) et seq.

many cities, considering the housing stock and economic constraints. This leads to suburbanization with its concomitant well-known ecological and administrative problems.

Consequently, substantial variances in the demand for properties in Germany are characteristic.[4] The high demand focuses primarily on metropoles and agglomerations, as well as on smaller university cities, which are deemed "attractive shortage cities."[5] Here, the issue of vacant apartments does not reveal itself in the shape of a lack in demand, but rather through a denial of offers, in order to generate higher returns, for instance through short-term letting to tourists. Legally, this is negotiated under the keyword *Zweckentfremdung* (misuse)[6] and is an issue of current legislation, but also an administrative problem of knowledge and enforcement. Accordingly, municipalities need to manage different problem areas, depending on the situation, and require a flexible set of instruments in terms of urban planning in order to do so.

4.2.2 Shrinking Cities and the Consequences

The regionally differentiated state of apartment vacancy ranks among the central consequences of urban planning of these shrink processes.[7] Generally speaking, there are more vacant apartments than private homes; there are, however, regional differences here as well.[8] An ongoing monitoring of vacancies is burdened with problems. Even the term itself is many-faceted.[9] It only partially occurs within the scope of official statistics. According to the census in 2011, the most recent comprehensive population survey, there are presently around 1.7 million vacant apartments in Germany.[10] Current predictions estimate that there will be a surplus of apartments between 3.3 and 4.5 million in 2030—which is not identical to a state of vacancy, but offers the nearest approach.[11] Long-term prognoses of developments like these are associated with extreme difficulties, as the migration processes both from within the and from outside the European Union show. Many assumptions have to be made regarding preferential decision-making of individual actors, which are influenced by a myriad of contextual factors. In that sense, one has to put the predictions—notwithstanding their indispensability—into perspective.[12] With these shrinking processes, continued maintenance of municipal and social infrastructure is in question.[13] The

[4]Bundesinstitut für Bau-, Stadt- und Raumforschung (2014a, b, p. 5).

[5]Bundesinstitut für Bau-, Stadt- und Raumforschung (2014a, b, p. 47).

[6]Cf. Ingold (2016, p. 595) et seq.

[7]Cf. Ingold (2016, p. 595) et seq.

[8]Bundesinstitut für Bau-, Stadt- und Raumforschung (2014a, b, p. 9).

[9]Bundesinstitut für Bau-, Stadt- und Raumforschung (2014a, b, p. 6).

[10]Bundesinstitut für Bau-, Stadt- und Raumforschung (2014a, b, p. 18).

[11]Bundesinstitut für Bau-, Stadt- und Raumforschung (2014a, b, p. 47).

[12]Bundesinstitut für Bau-, Stadt- und Raumforschung (2014a, b, p. 47).

[13]With regard to demographic change: Edenharter (2014, p. 61) et seq.

concept of local self-government, especially within the framework of municipal administrative autonomy, is facing major adjustment problems as well.

In recent years, urban planning legislation has been increasingly sensitized for these challenges. This is made clear by frequent changes to the BauGB (German Building Code) in comparatively short intervals.[14] The outlined framework conditions bring forth the ambivalence that urban planning legislation needs to make a contribution to the processing of an only roughly sketched out and regionally different problem, which cannot be solved solely by private actors nor by public administration.[15] At the same time, urban redevelopment is regulated and shaped through regulatory and incentive structures as well, which emerge from federal and European multi-level governance. Additionally, well-known coordination problems of differing expert planning processes are raised against the backdrop of administrative and political goals. To that extent, the law needs to structure cooperation and simultaneously attune itself to the respective procedural logics while also ensuring orientation towards public interest. This role is given to the urban planning development concept, among others.

4.3 Contours of the Development Concept as Regards Urban Planning

The urban planning development concept constitutes the central figure in construction law in the section on urban redevelopment, whose primary function is meant to be the management of shrinking processes in terms of planning law. Thus, the development concept as regards urban planning was designed with regard to apartment vacancies and the therefore necessary dismantling of housing stocks, as early as during legislative proceedings.[16] Later on, it became an increasingly multifunctional instrument of urban development with its subsequent extension for climate protection purposes,[17] whereas the instruments continue to stay largely geared toward management of the state of vacancy. Legal processing of the vacancy results from the regulatory context of urban redevelopment (3.1). Based on this foundation, the contours of the urban planning development concept can be outlined in greater detail (3.2). Ultimately, the aim is to understand the character of the urban planning development concept as a concept more closely (3.3).

---

[14]Strauß (2010). Chancen und Probleme der Informalität. In Bernt et al. (2010, p. 79) et seq. also refers to this development.

[15]Cf. also: Bernt et al. (2010). Stadtumbau als Problem der Governance-Forschung. In Bernt et al. (2010, p. 19).

[16]*Gesetzentwurf der Bundesregierung zur Anpassung des Baugesetzbuches an EU-Richtlinien* [Legal draft bill of the German Federal Government for adjustment of the German Building Code to EU-directives], BT-Drs. [German Bundestag (BT)-Documents (Drs.)] 15/2250:37, 60.

[17]Cf. Battis et al. (2010, p. 258) et seq.

4.3.1 *Urban Redevelopment as a Regulatory Context*

The normative reference point of the urban planning development concept is urban redevelopment. This way, with a change to the German building code in 2004, a former political-administrative term became a legal one.[18] It is meant to express the adjustment of urban structures to altered economic and demographic framework conditions without solely emphasizing the dismantling of vacant properties. Thus, a lasting impression has been made on the problem perspective.[19] Urban redevelopment is generally geared toward city and town districts. Therefore, the development concept's area of planning is situated between the development plan, which ordinarily regulates only a small part of the city, and the zoning plan that encompasses the entire municipal area. By Law/Legally, a permanent loss of function (in terms of urban planning) of a certain area is understood to be the requirement for urban redevelopment and for concepts that refer to it.[20] A leading legal example for such a loss of function is a continuous surplus of buildings, especially for residential purposes, in other words: vacant homes.[21] Such a structural[22] loss of function—as opposed to one referring to climate protection[23]—arises in particular from the comparison with planning determinations for a certain area.[24] Overall, municipalities are granted a broad scope of interpretation for defining whether there is a problem in this regard.

The goal of an urban redevelopment is the creation of sustainable structures of urban planning.[25] With this goal the guiding principle of urban development of § 1 par. 5 p. 1 BauGB is conceived and put into concrete terms. Such sustainable structures are characterized by the fact that they largely bring economic, ecological, and social aspects into conformity.[26] For this reason they enable future-oriented and future-proof development. In contrast, city districts affected by losses of function do not appear sustainable, as they prevent an economic focus of resources, seal areas that are not needed from an ecological perspective, and jeopardize social integration within an urban community. Normative guidelines for urban redevelopment have been determined by law as well, which vacillate between goals and measures in order

[18]Via the EAG Bau [European Law Adjustment Bill Building] 2004, for the background of its development cf. Krautzberger. In eds. Ernst, Zinkahn, Bielenberg (Status: 2012), preliminary note to §§ 171a to 171d, Rn. 12, pointing out that it is essentially a codification of the financing already practised within the federal urban development promotion programme.

[19]For an instructive analysis cf. Robinschon (2010). Stadtumbau als Begriff und politisches Deutungsmuster. In Bernt et al. (2010, p. 31) et seq.

[20]§ 171a par. 2 *BauGB*.

[21]§ 171a par. 2 p. 2 *BauGB*.

[22]Differentiation cf. Reidt (2019), in Battis et al. (2019), § 171a Rn. 2.

[23]Furthermore, a loss of function is assumed, provided that the adjustment to climate change does not occur.

[24]Reidt (2019), in Battis et al. (2019), § 171a Rn. 5.

[25]§ 171a par. 2 p. 1. *BauGB*.

[26]For the concept of sustainability in the German building law cf. e.g. Krautzberger (2001, p. 130).

to substantiate the goal of sustainable urban development.[27] This way, inner cities are meant to be strengthened and existing old buildings located there are supposed to stay unchanged, while buildings that are no longer meeting demands are to be either re-utilized or dismantled and vacant areas ought to be made available to be used in sustainable urban development.

Urban devolpment is related to[28] regarding both norm-structure and content.[29] These legal concepts have in common that they are intended for comprehensive and sustainable urban development. Reorganization law in particular played a pioneering role to the extent that it established this urban planning function alongside traditional construction planning and construction facilitation functions.[30] All these approaches exhibit the character of extensive urban development measures emerging from district-related issues. However, restructuring and development measures are precisely not geared towards processing the phenomenon of shrinking cities, thus, orchestrated differently.

4.3.2 Contours of the Urban Planning Development Concept

The urban planning development concept to manage states of vacancy is procedurally as well as materially only roughly pre-structured normatively. According to statutory conception, the concept's establishment is closely tied to the specification of the urban redevelopment area. The concept itself is intended to determine goals and measures, which counterbalance the loss of function of buildings. In doing so, it can incorporate the respective cities' particular logic, allowing for an equally integrated as well as strategic planning, for an equally integrated as well as strategic planning, which of course depends on previous decisions and self-descriptions.[31]

The procedure's introduction is not regulated. Generally speaking, the creation of such a concept should be decided on by the municipal representative body, not least because of regularly needed budgetary resources. The concept's content is comprised of urban planning goals that are defined for a specific area, however, unlike other plans, measures that pertain to those as well. Both affected parties and bodies responsible for public affairs are to partake in the drafts.[32] In what manner this occurs is left to municipal freedom to design the administrative procedure, unlike the way it is with urban development planning. The statutory mandate that participation

---

[27] § 171a par. 3 Nr. 1-7 *BauGB*. This ambivalence is also noted in: Robischon, Stadtumbau als Begriff und politisches Deutungsmuster. In Bernt et al. (2010, p. 37) et seq.; whereas legal literature does predominantly speak of goals in accordance with the text of the building law.

[28] Möller, in Schrödter (2015), § 171a Rn. 4.

[29] For the application of both legal systems in this context cf. Edenharter (2014, p. 410) et seq.

[30] Extensively on this matter cf. Schulze-Fielitz (1979).

[31] Formative in defining a concept of a specific inner logic for each city cf. Löw (2008, p. 65) et seq.; cf. also Kuder (2009). Pfadanalysen—ein Konzept zur Erforschung der Regenerierung von Städten. In Kühn and Liebmann (2009, p. 66) et seq.

[32] § 137, 139 *BauGB*.

of affected parties is ideally meant to be activated (§ 137 p. 2 BauGB) only expresses essential matters rudimentarily. In case of subsequent use, owners have to surrender their property in case of a dismantling of vacant home. Thus, an urban planning development concept can only be implemented if the rationale of the real estate market is incorporated. In this respect, a cooperative planning process is required. There are, of course, dangers that are connected to this.[33] There is need of actors who are willing and, especially, able to participate. Consequently and inevitably, a self-selection of participants occurs. In comparison to individual owners, housing companies are, generally speaking, more willing to engage in these processes, which may culminate in a one-sided orientation of development concepts.

Decisions on the urban planning development concept are made on the base of municipal regulations. In its final form, the decision on the development concept thus behooves the representative bodies. They have to carry out a planning assessment of the affected public and private interests.[34] Thus, doctrines of fair balance are generally established in tandem with the possibility of a judicial review of errors. The concept must be drawn up in writing, but is not subject to a disclosure obligation.[35] Even without any legal obligations, this is however the general practice because of the concept's function for municipal development and the activation of all involved actors alone. The accompanying decision on the determination of the urban redevelopment area opens up different courses of action for the municipality within the regulatory structures of urban planning and constitutes the prerequisite for participation in federal urban planning funding.[36] The changeability of established development concepts during their implementation is not pre-structured normatively, thus making it possible without limitations.[37] Due to a lack of a binding effect, a deviation of the municipality from the concept is possible at any time, even without alterations.[38] In doing so, the aim is to maintain the balance between learning ability and auditing, as well as the necessary planning reliability for the involved private actors.[39]

---

[33] For the following issue cf. Bernt et al. (2010, p. 24).

[34] § 171b par. 2 p. 2 *BauGB*.

[35] Reidt (2019) (n. 24), § 171b Rn. 2.

[36] Similarily cf. Reidt (2019) (n. 24), § 171b Rn. 2; cf. section IV.

[37] Compare Möller (2015) (n. 28), § 171b Rn. 4: adjustment as permanent task.

[38] Uechtritz (2010, p. 650) et seq.

[39] Critically Bernt et al. (2010, p. 25). The half-value time of development concepts only takes two to three years.

4.3.3 The Urban Planning Development Concept as a Concept

The urban planning development concept is part of the development toward "thinking conceptually"[40] in German administrative law. In a myriad of legal sectors, administrative concepts serve the self programming of public administration by now. They attract special attention in places where they are called upon, in order to bridge the gap between norms, which are describing only abstract goals, and individual decisions.[41] In the field of area and construction planning concepts are merely a limited innovation. This way, they bring back memories of urban development concepts encompassing all policy areas in the context of the planning euphoria from the 1970s.[42] But even in small-scale units like these, central public planning fails when faced with the interdependencies of municipal policies and the overestimation of public management of all social areas.[43] By contrast, urban planning development concepts are substantially more openly designed in terms of problem definition and implementation.[44] Also new is the urban planning formation as well as the connection to the federal grants scheme. The urban planning development concepts thus form a part in other options for municipalities to work with concepts,[45] which, irrespective of differences in the details, express the necessity to supplement the classic legally binding instruments of urban planning legislation. It would not be enough, however, to view the concepts' functions merely in the preparation of binding urban development planning.[46] This perspective is connected, of course, to legal classification and its difficulties.

In German administrative law, only urban land-use plans are given an external effect. To that extent, this sharp dichotomy between formal and informal planning differentiates according to the administrative type of action and its binding nature. Therefore, due to a lack of binding external effects, urban planning development concepts are legally accredited with the status of "informal planning." When dissociated from urban development planning, this may be perfectly understandable, but it is also at least misleading in regards to its legal significance and factual (pre-)effect.[47]

40Rixen (2014, p. 334).

41Herzmann (2013), Rottenwallner (2014).

42Originally, the term city development concept was intended for the government draft bill, which was only replaced by the designation urban planning development concept in the course of legislative procedures, cf. *Gesetzentwurf der Bundesregierung zur Anpassung des Baugesetzbuches an EU-Richtlinien* (n. 16), p. 60 and often-cited.

43On these problems in general at an early stage cf. Scharpf (1973). Komplexität als Schranke politischer Planung. In Scharpf (1973, p. 73) et seq.

44Cf. Kühn (2009), Strategische Planung—ein Ansatz zur Regenerierung schrumpfender Städte. In Kühn and Liebmann (2009, p. 85) et seq.

45Compare Winkler (2015).

46Uechtritz (2010, p. 647) et seq.

47Compare Möller (2015) (n. 28), § 171a Rn. 2: "Thus, the urban redevelopment concepts ought not to be understood and designated solely as "informal planning" or referred to on the base of their alleged non-binding nature."; very critical also *ibid.*, § 171b Rn. 5.

At any rate, there is no preference implied for legally binding tools.[48] As a consequence of the classification of the urban planning concept as informal planning, there is generally no possibility to obtain judicial review against the concept as such. An audit is only indirectly possible. As an assessment criterion, development concepts can have relevance for subsequent building plans.[49] A judicial control is therefore indirectly possible within the scope of a judicial review of a construction plan, which implements an urban planning development concept. So far, however, no pertinent decisions could be recorded. This fact stands opposite to the tremendous number of development concepts that can be found on the internet pages of the cities. It underlines the conceptual nature of these concepts in dealing with, inter alia, vacant homes from a local perspective.

There is a dilemma in the clear differentiation between legally binding and non-binding forms of action. On the one hand, such a demarcation is juristically inevitable. On the other hand, it appears to be unsatisfying in the long run. In part, the concepts are hence understood as a third category, characterized by an "indirect binding nature."[50] In legal literature, "informal planning"—as can be seen in the conceptualization—is understood as a weakness.[51] Vice versa, one is able to view it from the perspective of its advantages as well.[52] These include, for instance, its wide planning approach, which is not bound to the catalogue of land uses in the urban development planning law, and the freedom in designing the procedure, as well as the fact that not every step of the decision-making process suffers from the latent threat of a transition to legal or jurisdictional communication respectively.

4.4 The Urban Planning Development Concept in Urban Planning Regulatory Structures

The urban planning development concept as a concept without initial legal external effects requires an embedding into further regulations for its implementation. Apart from the general options of action in administrative and construction law, specific mechanisms may be carved out, which normatively account for the particularities of urban redevelopment. To that extent, the general legal principle is the contractually supported cooperation with the involved actors (4.1). This, however, remains in the

[48] Krautzberger and Stüer (2014, p. 1092): stressing the factual significance and the equality of informal planning.

[49] § 1 par. 6 Nr. 11 *BauGB*.

[50] But compare Krautzberger and Stüer (2014, p. 1092) (own translation): "This way, the BauGB avoids statutory standardization of a third, legally fleshed out planning level between regional plan and urban land-use plan or between zoning plan and development plan, respectively. Simultaneously, the BauGB assumes that urban planning actions, namely also urban development planning, are embedded into a mesh of informal planning."

[51] Cf. Winkler (2015, p. 473) et seq.

[52] Strauß (2010). Chancen und Probleme der Informalität. In Bernt et al. (2010, p. 79) et seq.

shadow of the hierarchy of different options in unilateral action (4.2). The imbedding into the federal distribution of funds reacts to the outlined particular economic conditions of urban redevelopment (4.3).

4.4.1 Cooperative Administrative Action as the Desired Outcome

The BauGB stipulates a normative preference for a cooperative implementation of the urban planning development concept.[53] This is orchestrated through the urban redevelopment contract.[54] The implementation of a complex development concept through a myriad of contracts that relate to one another hereby poses immense requirements for the organization and coordination of administration.[55] Legally, it is a specific use of the urban planning contract which is foreseen as a tool in § 11 BauGB. Its general requirements, namely the *quid pro quo* principle and the prohibition to link the contract with other affairs of these parties, apply to urban redevelopment contracts to that extent as well.[56] Judicial protection in administrative law against the contracts is established to the extent that it may lead to incident reviews of the development concept.

Three constellations are typified legally as examples, which showcase the application of urban redevelopment contracts:[57] Firstly, a dismantling of specific properties such as vacant ones may be agreed upon, including payment of costs. This means factually that either the municipality bears the costs or, predominantly, that the federal funding for the city's redevelopment, which requires respective co-financing, may be passed on and amended contractually. Secondly, as typical regulatory content, the waiver of compensation claims acc. §§ 39–44 BauGB for losing the possibility of the using the buildings is stipulated. This may be understood as an adjustment of the conception of the urban development planning to the specific economic logic of the urban redevelopment. An area, which became vacant due to dismantling, is oftentimes planned for to the effect that its building potential is revoked or strongly limited. Compensation claims of the BauGB, intended for constellations like these, appear to be hardly appropriate, when a dismantling of existing buildings has been primarily funded publically in the past. Thirdly, an equal distribution of burdens between affected proprietors may be stipulated in an urban redevelopment contract. At any rate, the problems of collective action may be lessened by this mechanism.[58]

---

[53]Cf. also Reidt (2019) (n. 24), § 171b Rn. 2§ 171c Rn. 1: legal principle; Möller (2015) (n. 28), § 171c Rn. 2: consensual principle stressed.

[54]§ 171c *BauGB*.

[55]Cf. Dürsch and Rixner (2018), § 171c Rn. 11 et seq.

[56]Cf. in detail Möller (2015) (n. 28), § 171a Rn. 10 et seq.

[57]§ 171c par. 2 Nr. 1–3 *BauGB*.

[58]For possibilities and modalities of the equalisation of burdens cf. Goldtschmidt and Taubenek (2010, p. 316) et seq.

This may be realized through the fact that a remaining proprietor learning about an increase in value through urban redevelopment makes a compensation payment to the municipality, which then pays out said payment to a proprietor, whose unit is to be dismantled. The probability of a contractual compensation of the different interests for the purpose of realizing the urban planning development concept are, at any rate, secured through the fact that they are meant to stand above an alternative usage of hierarchical actions of public authorities.

4.4.2 The Shadow of Hierarchy in Construction Law

The urban redevelopment contract as a standard procedure of implementation lies, however, in the shadow of the hierarchy[59] of other courses of action in construction law.[60] First, the realization of an urban planning development concept can be secured through binding urban redevelopment statutes.[61] In the light of procedures connected to this, prerequisite for a statute ordinance is that the options of a consensual implementation of the development concept have failed.[62] This opens up the possibility of a "freeze" for any development in urban redevelopment law. On the basis of the statute, undertakings that are subject to authorization in the defined urban redevelopment area or in a part of it may be declined and those not requiring authorization, including dismantling of vacant homes, may be put under a governmental provision of approval. Then, the prerequisite for an approval is the fact that the project does not jeopardize the urban redevelopment measures on the base of the development concept.[63] The urban redevelopment statute opens up possibilities of the right of for the city to buy the land when the owner wants to sell it to third parties and expropriation as well.[64] This exemplifies the primacy of consensual solutions. Only if these fail, interventions through expropriation or the right of first refusal may be justified, respectively. Judicial protection against an urban redevelopment statute is established through the review of the administrative court acc. § 47 VwGO (German Rules forAdministrative Courts). As the statute serves the safeguarding of the urban planning development concept, the implicit monitoring of the development concept is connected therewith, as well as considerations that were made at this point. Overall,

---

[59]For the term cf. Scharpf (1991, p. 629).

[60]Möller (2015) (n. 28), § 171a Rn. 3: stating that urban redevelopment statutes enable the administration of subordinate sovereign intervention.

[61]§ 171 d *BauGB*.

[62]Möller (2015) (n. 28), § 171a Rn. 5.

[63]In detail cf. Roesner (2014). In: Schlichter et al. (2014), § 171d Rn. 11 et seq.; Schmidt-Eichstaedt, in Brügelmann (2016), § 171d Rn. 16 et seq.

[64]§§ 24 par. 1 Nr. 4, 25 par. 1 Nr. 2 (rights of pre-emption) 85 par. 1 Nr. 7; cf. Krautzberger (2012). In Ernst, Zinkahn, Bielenberg & Krautzberger, Preliminary note to §§ 171a bis 171d, Rn. 7.

the urban redevelopment statute is essentially a passive-reactive management instrument of the municipality, which allows for possibilities of intervention, but does not enable a positive design of the urban redevelopment.[65]

Moreover, possibilities for a one-sided municipal order to dismantle of structures, i.e. vacant residential properties, arise from regulations in building planning law and federal state building order. First, urban planning directives acc. § 175 et seqq. BauGB may be employed.[66] The dismantling decree of § 179 BauGB provides for two alternatives. Claims for compensation are regularized acc. § 179 par. 3, 4 BauGB, but the use of this option is less attractive from a municipal perspective. By contrast, the building law regulations of many federal states stipulate a dismantling decree without compensation.[67] However, there are very narrow prerequisites for this alternative. Additionally, further legal options for administrative action may arise for so-called junk real estates, which violate safety regulations.[68]

4.4.3 *Urban Planning Development Concepts in the Municipal Funding Regime*

Urban planning development concepts only unfold their actual effect in the context of urban planning funding through the federal government.[69] This is integrated into the cooperative federalism, which is characteristic for Germany. It occurs on the base of art. 104b GG (German Constitutional Law) i.c.w. § 164b BauGB and is orchestrated through an annually reissued administrative agreement between the federal government and the federal states.[70] With respect to the urban development policy's structure of competences, these funding programmes are the essential design instrument of the federal government, apart from providing the urban planning framework within the building code. It exhibits structural similarities to the access of the European Union, which seeks to influence sustainable urban development through the co-financing of projects within the scope of its structural funding.[71] In that sense,

[65] Möller (2015) (n. 28), § 171d Rn. 1 et seq.

[66] In detail cf. Edenharter (2014, p. 451) et seq.

[67] Exemplarily cf. § 80 par. 2 Brandenburgische Bauordnung: "The building supervisory authority may order the removal of a structural installation even at times, when it is not being used and its dilapidation is impending and there is no public interest or private interest in its preservation worthy of protection." More details on this and on parallel provisions of state legislation cf. Guckelberger (2010, p. 743) et seq.

[68] Compare Bundesministerium für Umwelt, Naturschutz und Reaktorsicherheit (2014).

[69] Also compare Möller (2015) (n. 28), § 171a Rn. 1: Regulations do have first and foremost funding law significance.

[70] Verwaltungsvereinbarung Städtebauförderung 2016 über die Gewährung von Finanzhilfen des Bundes an die Länder nach Artikel 104b des Grundgesetzes zur Förderung städtebaulicher Maßnahmen (*VV Städtebauförderung 2016*) vom 18.12.2015/15.03.2016.

[71] Cf. art. 7 of the regulation (EU) No. 1301/2013 of the European Parliament for regional development and with particular regulations in regard to the goal "Investments in growth and employment"

the prima facie municipal problem of vacant homes is extensively embedded into the German and European multi-level governance.[72]

In the course of urban construction funding of the federal government, the funding of measures of urban redevelopment comprises almost a third of the current annual funding sum with 200 million Euros.[73] In the administrative agreement governing this funding, the federal states are each obligated to present state programmes for the funding of urban planning, in order to be eligible to make use of financial aids.[74] The allocation procedure is predominantly left to these state programmes. One of the few funding prerequisites already formulated in the administrative agreement is the presentation of an urban planning development concept.[75] This, too, is important from the perspective of funding ministry, in order to be able to link adjusted and consensual planning to the respective needs. The establishment of the concept and its further development, can also be funded. An explicit emphasis is put on the cimprehensive character of these concepts, which are meant to go beyond simple dismantling. In the course of this, application criteria for such funding have retroactive effects on strategic behavior and should thus already influence the creation of urban planning development concepts. Funding criteria of urban redevelopment are thereby accused of being too strongly geared toward the needs of the housing market.[76] From a perspective of administrative science, application-oriented funding programmes are furthermore attested to have undeceivable deadweight effects.[77]

The administrative agreement does not institutionalize a competition between the federal states in order to get funding, but rather sets up a proportionate distribution of financial resources to the individual federal states. This occurs via indicators which are tied to the shrinking process. The federal states do not open up a competition of funding resources either, but rather demand municipal applications and thus count on negotiations as a mode of coordination. The programme is fundamentally geared toward co-financing. Funding for dismantling in East Germany turns out especially high and is, moreover, subject to the condition that the states completely take on the necessary co-financing.[78]

---

and the abrogation of regulation (EG) No. 1080/2006, *ABl.* 2013 L 347/289: financial support of the European Union for projects of sustainable urban development through strategies with integrated measures to manage the economic, ecological, climatic, demographic, and social challenges urban areas are confronted with.

[72]Cf. Kilper (2009). Multilevel Governance—Anregungen für die Analyse von Stadtentwicklungspolitik in schrumpfenden Städten. In Kühn and Liebmann (2009, p. 109) et seq.

[73]Cf. the allocation of means in art. 1 par. 2 *VV Städtebauförderung 2016.*

[74]Art. 10 *VV Städtebauförderung 2016*: federal state programmes are compulsory; Art. 21 *VV Städtebauförderung 2016*: funding regulations of the federal states are compulsory.

[75]Art. 5 par. 1 *VV Städtebauförderung 2016.*

[76]Bernt, and Haus, Stadtumbau als Problem der Governance-Forschung. In Bernt et al. (2010, p. 25) et seq.

[77]Bogumil (2011, p. 86).

[78]Art. 2 *VV Städtebauförderung 2016.*

4.5 Conclusion and Outlook

The urban development concept and the urban redevelopment areas comprise the essential urban planning reaction to the shrinking processes of cities. They are intended to offer a flexible instrument for the municipal shaping of this transformation. This is expressed primarily in the fact that legal regulations are geared toward cooperative and consensual administrative action. One-sided action is intended to be merely subordinate and serves not least as a promotor of consensual action. The execution of such norms is significantly determined by their integration into urban development funding by the federal government. Only through the eligibility conditions of an urban planning development concept did it become a municipal standard in the managing of vacancies in Germany.

References

Battis U, Kersten J, Mitschang S (2010) Klimaschützende Stadterneuerung, *ZG* 2010:246–259
Battis U, Krautzberger M, Löhr R-P (2019) Baugesetzbuch, 14th edn. Beck, München
Bernt M, Haus M, Robischon T (eds) (2010) Stadtumbau komplex: Governance, Planung, Prozess. Schader-Stiftung, Darmstadt
Bogumil J (2011) Möglichkeiten und Grenzen nationaler Stadtpolitik. In: Hanesch W (ed) Die Zukunft der "Sozialen Stadt". VS Verlag fuer Sozialwissenschaften, Wiesbaden, pp 81–95
Brügelmann H (Status: 2016) *BauGB*, München: Beck
Bundesinstitut für Bau-, Stadt- und Raumforschung (2014a) *Aktuelle und zukünftige Entwicklung von Wohnungsleerständen in den Teilräumen Deutschlands*
Bundesinstitut für Bau-, Stadt- und Raumforschung (2014b) *Entwicklung von Wohnungsleerständen*
Bundesministerium für Umwelt, Naturschutz und Reaktorsicherheit (2014) *Verwahrloste Immobilien*
Dürsch H-P, Rixner F (2018) In: Rixner F et al (eds) Systematischer Praxiskommentar BauGB/BauNVO, 3rd edn (§ 171c Rn. 11 et seq.)
Edenharter A (2014) *Der demographische Wandel als Herausforderung für das Raumordnungsrecht und das Baurecht*. Duncker & Humblot, Berlin
Ernst W, Zinkahn W, Bielenberg W, Krautzberger M (Status: 2012) *BauGB*, München: Beck
Goldtschmidt J, Taubenek O (2010) Stadtumbau. Beck, München
Guckelberger A (2010) Abbruch verfallender baulicher Anlagen. NVwZ 2010:743–748
Herzmann K (2013) Was sind administrative Konzepte. VerwArch 2013:429–448
Ingold A (2016) Die "Sharing Economy" der kurzzeitigen Unterkunftsvermietung als Herausforderung für das Gewerbe-, Bau- und Ordnungsrecht. DÖV 2016:595–603
Kilper H (2009) Multilevel Governance—Anregungen für die Analyse von Stadtentwicklungspolitik in schrumpfenden Städten. In: Kühn M, Liebmann H (eds) Regenerierung schrumpfender Städte, pp 109–122
Krautzberger M (2001) Nachhaltige Entwicklung und Städtebaurechtsordnung. UPR 2001:130–133
Krautzberger M (2012) Preliminary Note to §§ 171a-d. In: Ernst W, Zinkahn W, Bielenberg W, Krautzberger M (eds) BauGB
Krautzberger M, Stüer B (2014) Städtebaurecht: Gestaltung des demographischen Wandels als Verwaltungsaufgabe. DVBl 2014:1085–1095
Kühn M, Liebmann H (eds) (2009) Regenierung schrumpfender Städte. VS Verlag für Sozialwissenschaften, Wiesbaden
Löw M (2008) Soziologie der Städte. Suhrkamp, Frankfurt am Main

Möller A (2015) §§ 171 a-d. In: Schrödter W (ed) BauGB
Reidt O (2019) § 171a-d. In: Battis U, Krautzberger M, Löhr R-P (eds) BauGB
Richardson HW, Nam CW (eds) (2014) Shrinking cities: a global perspective. Routledge, London
Rixen S (2015) Gestaltung des demographischen Wandels als Verwaltungsaufgabe. VVDStRL 74:293–350
Robinschon T (2010) Stadtumbau als Begriff und politisches Deutungsmuster. In: Bernt M, Haus M, Robinschon T (eds) Stadtumbau komplex: Governance, Planung, Prozess, pp 30–43
Roesner V (2014) §§ 171a-d. In: Schlichter O, Stich R, Driehaus H-J, Paetow S (eds) BauGB
Rottenwallner T (2014) Die Konzepte und Konzeptpflichten der öffentlichen Verwaltung. In *VR* 2014:109–122
Scharpf F (1973). *Planung als politischer Prozess* Frankfurt (Main): Suhrkamp
Scharpf F (1991) Die Handlungsfähigkeit des Staates am Ende des 20. Jahrhunderts, Politische Vierteljahresschrift 32:621–634
Schlichter O, Stich R, Driehaus H-J, Paetow S (eds) (Status:2014), *Berliner Kommentar zum Baugesetzbuch (BauGB),* München:Beck
Schulze-Fielitz H (1979) Sozialplanung im Städtebaurecht. Athenäum, Königstein/TS
Schrödter W (ed) (2015) *BauGB* (8th edn.), München: Beck
Strauß C (2010) Chancen und Probleme der Informalität. In Bernt M, Haus M, Robinschon T (eds) Stadtumbau komplex, pp 78–93
Uechtritz M (2010) Die Bedeutung informeller Planungen für die Bauleitplanung und für Genehmigungsentscheidungen. ZfBR 2010:646–653
Winkler M (2015). Vom Bauleitplan zum "Masterplan": Informelle Konzepte im Baurecht. In: Geis M-E, Winkler M, Bickenbach C (eds) *Von der Kultur der Verfassung: Festschrift für Friedhelm Hufen zum 70. Geburtstag*, pp 573–584

Chapter 5
The Tragedies of the Commons and Anticommons in an Era of Underuse

Abstract Japan's Land Use Law and City Planning Law have traditionally focused on addressing the issue of an "urbanizing society" and the "overuse" brought on by population growth and economic growth. However, in an "urbanized society" where urban expansion has subsided, legal responses to new issues such as landscape problems and area management will be necessary. In addition, the problem of unoccupied houses and unclaimed land brought about by an age of population decline indicates that legal measures to address "underuse" are becoming increasingly important. This chapter examines recent Japanese legal responses to challenges in an era of "underuse" from the perspective of the "tragedy of the commons" presented by G. Hardin and the "tragedy of the anti-commons" presented by M. Heller.

Keywords Underuse · The tragedy of commons · The tragedy of anticommons · Landscape · Area management · Unclaimed land · Owner-unknown land

5.1 Introduction

Japan's Land Use Law and City Planning Law have traditionally focused on addressing the "urbanizing society" and "overuse" brought on by population growth and economic growth. However, in an "urbanized society" where urban expansion has subsided, legal responses to new issues such as landscape problem and area management will be necessary. In addition, the problem of unoccupied houses and unclaimed land brought about by the age of population decline indicates that legal measures to address "underuse" are becoming increasingly important.

This chapter is based on the author's presentation at the international workshop "A Cooperative Establishment in a Downscaling Society" (Mar.14, 2018, Chonbuk National University, Korea). The Japanese version is published as "*Kashō Riyō Jidai ni okeru Komonzu no Higeki to Antikomonzu no Higeki*" (The tragedy of commons and the tragedy of anticommons in an era of underuse), in M. Noro et al. (eds), Gendai Gyōsei to Nettowāku Riron (Hōritsubunkasha, 2019), pp. 143–170. This work was supported by JSPS KAKENHI Grant Numbers JP26285009, JP15H03290, JP18H00796, JP18KK0033. The author would like to thank Gengo Inc. for the provisional translation and Dr. Steve Pickering (Brunel University London) for great editing.

N. Kadomatsu et al., *Legal Responses to Vacant Houses*,
Kobe University Social Science Research Series,
https://doi.org/10.1007/978-981-15-6641-7_5

This chapter examines recent Japanese legal responses to challenges in an era of "underuse" from the perspective of the "tragedy of the commons" presented by G. Hardin and the "tragedy of the anti-commons" presented by M. Heller.

Section 1 discusses Hardin's "tragedy of the commons" argument as a justification for property rights, pointing out the distinction between "literal commons" and "figurative commons" and the distinction between the three solutions ("solution through property rights", "rule-based solution", and "solution through collective management") (1.1). From this point of view, we will examine "landscape as commons" (1.2) and the legal measures toward "area management" (1.3), both of which have become important legal issues in Japan since the 2000s.

Section 2 analyzes the Japanese Supreme Court's "Forest Law Judgment" in 1987 (2.2) in terms of Heller's "tragedy of the anticommons" argument (2.1). From this perspective, I will examine the recent legislative measures toward the "unclaimed land" problem (2.3), which symbolizes the era of underuse. Particular emphasis will be placed on the theoretical implications of the "undertakings for the promotion of welfare of the community", stipulated in the Unclaimed Land Act of 2018 (2.4).

5.2 The Tragedy of the Commons

5.2.1 The "Tragedy of the Commons" as a Justification for the Property Rights System

In general, there are two ways in which the property rights system is justified. The first emphasizes the protection of personal freedoms as the function of property rights; in other words, the focus is on securing the stable existence of the holder of the property rights and achieving the physical requirements for personal freedom. The second line of reasoning involves distributing resources by dividing up the property rights among various stakeholders; this logic pursues greater efficiency in the use of the resources and seeks to enhance the welfare of society as a whole.

We will temporarily put aside the first line of reasoning and first focus on the postulation of the "tragedy of the commons" by Garett Hardin. He paints a picture which can be summarized as below.

> There is a pasture open to all. Various herdsman let their cattle to graze on this pasture and determine the number of cattle based upon their own costs and benefits. If a given herdsman puts more livestock on the pasture, the benefit will be exclusively attributed to the owner but the cost (deterioration of the pasture by overgrazing) are shared by all the herdsmen. Therefore, the only sensible course for each herdsman is to add more cattle on the pasture. As a result, too much cattle are turned loose, and no herdsman is able to maintain his own cattle, and no one ends up with their desired result. In order to avoid this tragedy, the common pasture will be divided into parcels and exclusive right of usage attributed to each herdsman.[1]

[1] Hardin (1968).

However, there are a few key points to consider here. Firstly, take the "pasture open to all" that Hardin presupposes—what is the actual nature of this pasture as a good? In the sense that it would be difficult to block external parties from using the pasture and other herdsmen from overusing it, it has a low level of exclusivity and is in a state of "open access." By contrast, it has competitiveness, in the sense that the more users of the pasture there are, the more the resources are consumed.[2] In other words, this is a "common pool" resource, to use the term coined by Elinor Ostrom.[3] If we look at the actual use of land in Japan for the purpose of attaining resources derived from the land, there are few plots that feature this element of a "common pool" resource. There is generally no "unowned" land, with all land largely having property rights associated with some public or private body. Therefore, in Japan, land for free productive use by anyone is nearly non-existent. Hardin's example presupposes a world in which property rights do not exist. Today, it belongs to the domain of the "fable."

That being said, there are more than a few cases of phenomena resembling the tragedy of the commons, such as management of fishery resources, global warming through energy consumption, traffic congestion, and other domains beyond physical land itself, where establishing property rights would prove difficult or impossible.[4] Returning to the subject of land proper, there are also similar examples to be found in illegal dumping in the context of vacant land that has an owner, but is substantively unmanaged, and in children's parks that are not maintained by anyone. Hardin also touches on environmental pollution and, as its cause, population growth, saying: "Here it is not a question of taking something out of the commons, but of putting something in".[5] Herein, I will treat the state of open access associated with the use of land as a resource, as in the case of the pasture above, as the "**literal commons**," and the state of open access for non-land phenomena or for purposes other than the use of resources as the "**figurative commons**."

Hardin goes on to suggest methods beyond the creation of property rights as a means of solving the tragedy of the commons. He states that in order to prevent the destruction of a national park due to increased visitors, we could (1) "sell them off as private property" or (2) "keep them as public property, but allocate the right to enter them." Allocating the right to enter the parks could involve various possibilities, among them (i) auction of the allocation rights (ii) allocation through merit-based standards (iii) lottery or (iv) first-come, first-served schemes, or other methods.[6]

For the sake of argument, I will refer to (1) as a "**solution through property rights**" and (2) as a "**rule-based solution**." In the case of (2), we would presume that (a) the government functions as the body enacting and executing these rules.

---

[2]There are other types of property rights, such as intellectual property, which lack this aspect of competitiveness.

[3]Ostrom (1990).

[4]Hardin himself cites the example of free parking in the Christmas shopping season, fishery resources and use of national parks. Hardin (1968, p. 1245).

[5]Hardin (1968, p. 1245).

[6]Hardin (1968, p. 1245).

However, (and Hardin may not have accounted for this) it would also be logically possible for (b) an autonomous group consisting of the herdsmen to manage the pasture. Among commons researchers, many emphasize the notion that it would be possible for a local society to collectively or autonomously manage shared spaces in a sustainable fashion, or at least it was possible at a certain time. These researchers have come to be referred to as "comedy of the commons theorists."[7]

In the above example, what led to the impoverishment of the common pasture was that, from the point of view of individual herdsman as operators, it was "reasonable" to allow for "just one more" head of cattle. If the individual herdsmen were not treated as managers, but rather a company collectively founded by them were the managing body, the entirety of the pasture would be looked at from the long-term view of maximizing its benefits, allowing for thinking about how to manage it sustainably. At least as a logical possibility, this would represent another way of solving the tragedy of the commons. I will refer to this as (3) **solution through collective management**.

5.2.2 Landscape as Commons

Around the 2000s in Japan, there was a sudden and marked interest in jurisprudence in the context of "landscapes." In 2004, the Landscape Act[8] was established. The impetus for this was the "*Kunitachi* condominium conflict" in *Kunitachi* City, Tokyo.[9] This incident involved a plan to construct an apartment complex approximately 40 meters tall alongside *Daigaku-dōri,* a street emblematic of community development and city planning in *Kunitachi.* The City Planning Act[10] and Building Standards Act[11] of the time allowed for apartment buildings of this height, but local residents felt that the height of the mansion would not coalesce with the rows of gingko and cherry trees along *Daigaku-dōri*, which had a height of 20 meters, so this would disrupt the landscape. The city government rapidly moved to create a district plan restricting the height of buildings to 20 meters, as well as ratify a set of building ordinances that would give legal force to said plan. However, the Tokyo metropolitan government, which has jurisdiction over the Building Standards Act, held that the apartments in question were already "under construction" (Article 3, Clause 2 of the Building Standards Act) on the date the *Kunitachi* regulations went into effect, so the district plan and ordinances did not apply to this complex (grandfather clause). Since Tokyo government took the stance of allowing a building of 40 meters in height, the neighboring residents lodged a suit. There are many cases of litigation, but two suits are worth mentioning here. Namely, (1) a civil litigation was lodged seeking an injunction against the construction of parts exceeding 40 meters in height (or for the

[7]E.g. Rose (1986). Cf. Takamura (2012, p. 7), Suga (2008).

[8]*Keikan Hō* (Act No. 110 of 2004).

[9]Regarding this conflict in general, see Kadomatsu (2017).

[10]*Toshi Keikaku Hō* (Act No. 100 of 1968).

[11]*Kenchiku Kijun Hō* (Act No. 201 of 1950).

removal of parts already constructed) and (2) administrative litigation was sought, asking that the aforementioned district plan and building ordinances be applied to the apartment, seeking Tokyo to issue an order barring construction of parts exceeding 40 meters (or an order for removal of parts already constructed).

In this case, both the judgment of first instance in the administrative litigation[12] and the judgment of first instance in the civil litigation[13] which upholded the residents' claims, made the following opinions, which treat the landscape as commons.[14] Both the appeals judgment in both suits and the Supreme Court judgment in the civil litigation[15] dismissed the claims of the residents, however.

[Judgment of first instance in administrative litigation (Judgment of the Tokyo District Court, December 4, 2001)] (hereafter" the Judgment A")

> For passersby, landscapes represent merely a one-way form of enjoyment; however, where buildings are one of the major constituent parts of a specific landscape, the persons residing within that space and those persons possessing buildings within said space, namely, users of the space, must maintain the aspects of the landscape in order to enjoy its benefits as intended. Furthermore, in cases such as these, if a particular user of one aspect forming the landscape does not follow the rules for its maintenance, there is a high likelihood of the landscape being immediately destroyed; unless all users of the landscape reciprocally maintain and respect it, the benefits conferred by said landscape cannot be enjoyed in a continuous manner. In other words, the maintenance of a landscape is only possible when all constituent and actual users of the landscape respect it; landscapes are highly dependent on a shared consciousness among their users.

[Judgment of first instance in civil suit: Judgment of the Tokyo District Court, December 18, 2002] (hereafter "the Judgment B")

> There are cases in which the property right holders establish certain standards on height, color or design for the buildings within the area and thus a certain landscape of the area evolves. When not only the residents but also the society at large considers it to be a good landscape, it gives added value to the lot. Such added value of urban landscape is by its nature different from enjoyment of the natural landscape of mountains or coast, or from enjoyment of historical buildings which are preserved at a cost to their owners. It is the property-right holders who enjoy the added value of the landscape themselves that have brought forth the value by their continuous effort. It required their mutual understanding, solidarity and self-sacrifice. In order to maintain such added value, the above standards must be observed by all the property-right holders. Only one property-right holder can immediately destroy the uniformity of the landscape by a building that violates the standard and deprives other property-right holders of the above added value.

With respect to the landscape as commons, we could interpret the above as follows. Seeking to avoid Hardin's tragedy of the commons, the law has created property rights through a two-layer division of space which involves (1) individually dividing up land that would otherwise be contiguous and (2) stipulating that property rights to land extend both above and below the surface of the land (Japanese Civil Code, article

[12]Judgment of the Tokyo District Court, December 4, 2001, *Hanrei Jihō* 1791:3.

[13]Judgment of the Tokyo District Court, December 18, 2002, *Hanrei Jihō* 1829:36.

[14]See also Kadomatsu (2017).

[15]The Supreme Court did not render a substantive decision on the administrative litigation.

207). However, by their nature, landscapes cannot be physically subdivided. Furthermore, they are a good in which, provided all recipients of the benefits conferred by a landscape use it while observing its rules with due care and maintain it as necessary, the landscape can confer major benefits on each person in a continuous fashion, but if a small subset of users pursue self-interest in a short-sighted manner, the landscape may be easily destroyed.[16] As people's interest in and the economic importance of a landscape grows, the tragedy of the commons effect once again is produced.

The unique aspect of these two judgments is that they found local residents (the plaintiffs) to bear a certain role in enforcing rules to preserve the landscape. Specifically, the Judgment A stated as follows, finding the plaintiffs having the standing to sue in order to enforce administrative and legal rules stipulated in district plans and building ordinances.

> "Owners of land in the district subject to height restrictions are…subject to the building ordinances and district plan which respectively impose a limit of 10 meters and 20 meters on buildings constructed in said district; landowners in the height-restricted district are users of the space encompassing *Daigaku-dōri* and exist in a **reciprocal interest relationship** whereby, by following the height restriction and by being subject to it, enjoy specific benefits conferred by the landscape of the aforementioned *Daigaku-dōri*...taking these factors into account, the building ordinance and Article 68, Clause 2 of the Building Standards Act achieve the public aim of maintaining the specific landscape of *Daigaku-dōri*. In addition, the building ordinances subject the landowners subject to building height restrictions in the district to other specific restrictions, which can be interpreted to impel each individual member to maintain and uphold those restrictions for the individual benefit of enjoying the landscape of *Daigaku-dōri*……"

The Judgment B also found that where (a) there is the ongoing application of self-imposed restrictions on the use of land by the landowners of a specific region, (b) a specific manmade landscape is maintained for a suitable length of time and that landscape is deemed good as per social norms, and (c) this landscape creates added value to the land owned by the landowners,

> "While the landowners of land in the region bear the obligation to exercise self-restraint on the free exercise of their own property rights, they must also seek the same obligation of other equivalent landowners."

In other words, the Judgment B finds that, irrespective of administrative regulations, there is an unwritten law of self-restraint (customary law, as it were) governing landowners in their use of the commons; for this reason, the courts found that there is a "interest in landscape" under legal protection of civil tort law. Based on this "interest in landscape," it acknowledged the local residents' right to seek an injunction against the construction of a building violating the above rules.

What this example of the "landscape as commons" has to teach us is, firstly, even where the "literal commons" is nonexistent and the land divided up, there may be cases where a "figurative commons" emerges as the point at issue due to economic/social conditions and changes in people's consciousness. Secondly, avoiding the tragedy of the commons would require re-dividing the "figurative

[16]Takamura (2012, p. 3).

commons" (a solution by use of property rights) or treating it as a commons and setting rules for the management thereof (a solution through rules). The latter brings up the third consequence, which is that a sort of interest-based collective is produced among the stakeholders in the commons (i.e., the "reciprocal relationship" referred to in the judgment of first instance in the administrative litigation proceedings). Thus, there are cases where the constituent members of that collective body are recognized to have certain privileges—both in terms of individual "rights" and a certain "competence" in managing the collective—to enforce the aforementioned rules.

5.2.3 Area Management as Management of the Commons

In recent years, a form of "area management" towards maintaining and improving a positive environment and local value through autonomous initiatives by residents, business operators, and landowners has drawn more attention. These initiatives include the holding of events to vitalize the region, engaging in cleanup activities, and the creation of autonomous community building rules. These area management initiatives can also be interpreted as cases where a given region or space, or the individual facilities or activities within it, are treated as a commons, with a body comprising local stakeholders being in charge of its management—corresponding to 3) above (see 1.1), namely, a "solution through collective management".

Some issues that occur when trying to justify the legal basis for area management activities in the management of the commons are (a) in which cases to formally (publicly) authorize area management and how to define the main agent (the area management body) for said activities, the spatial scope, and the scope of stakeholders therein (**authorization of area and agent**); (b) how to allocate the burden of costs for these activities, and whether to levy their collection (prevention of free riders) (**costs allocation**); and (c) whether it is possible to enforce the payment of dues and observance of autonomous community building rules in stakeholders who have not consented to said activities (**necessity of consent**).[17]

In 2014, Osaka City enacted a new local ordinance (*Ōsaka Shi Eria Manejiment Katsudō Sokushin Jōrei* [Osaka City Area Management Promotion Ordinance], hereafter "Osaka Ordinance"). The ordinance is the first attempt in Japan to introduce a comprehensive legal scheme of Business Improvement Districts (BIDs), which is widely utilized in North America and Europe.

Under the Osaka BID scheme the city mayor may designate area management bodies as "Urban Reconstruction promotion corporations" stipulated in Article 118 of the Act on Special Measures concerning Urban Reconstruction[18] (*Toshi Saisei Tokubetsu Sochi Hō*, hereafter the "Urban Reconstruction Act") and may certify the "district management plan" proposed by the area management body (Article 2, Osaka Ordinance) ((a) **authorization of area and agent**).

---

[17] See Kadomatsu (2018).

[18] Act No. 22 of 2002.

The Osaka ordinance also makes it possible for area management organizations to collect contributions from the beneficiaries of the activities and use the collected funds as the subsidies for area management activities. For that purpose, the ordinance utilizes a levy scheme (*Buntankin*) in the Article 224 of the Local Autonomy Act. However, the purpose of the subsidy is limited to the maintenance and management of certain public facilities designated under the Urban Reconstruction Act (Article 46, para 16. "Urban Convenience Promotion Facilities" (*Toshi Riben Zōshin Shisetsu*) ((b) **costs allocation**).

However, the premise of the application of the BID scheme is the conclusion of the Urban Convenience Promotion Agreement (*Toshi Riben Zōshin Kyōtei*) in Article 74 of the Urban Reconstruction Act. Such agreements shall be voluntarily concluded between the area management organization and the landowners or leaseholders. Namely, the collection of compulsory contributions is possible only from those beneficiaries that have voluntarily agreed in advance to pay the contributions. Thus the only merit of using the scheme is that the collection of the money will be conducted by local governments, which nevertheless has significance[19] ((c) **necessity of consent**).

In June 2018, two important revisions of the laws were enacted concerning area management. These are an amendment to the Local Revitalization Act (*Chiiki Saisei Ho*[20]), which falls under the jurisdiction of the Cabinet Office, and an amendment to the Urban Reconstruction Act, which falls under the jurisdiction of the Ministry of Land, Infrastructure, Transport, and Tourism.

The amendment to the Local Revitalization Act involves, like the Osaka ordinance, the introduction of a BIDs system. It defines area management activities carried out in "a given region, as based on natural, economic, or social factors" where the expectation of increased tourists to the region will lead to more employment opportunities and the expansion of the economic base as "activities for the increased convenience of local visitors". Area management bodies, which carry out activities to improve the convenience of visitors to the local region, can file with the local mayor for approval of a plan (Local Tourists Convenience Promotion Action Plan*(Chiiki Raihōshatō Riben Zōshin Katsudō Keikaku)* that describes these activities ((a) **authorization of area and agent**). One requirement to file for approval is a 2/3 majority of beneficiary businesses of the activities and a similar 2/3 majority for the allocation of expenses.Where the action plan is approved, the local mayor can levy expenses from the beneficiary businesses of the activities and use this as a subsidy for the area management body ((b) **costs allocation**). Unique aspects of this amendment are the way it (1) treats the scope of stakeholders as business operators (rather than landowners or residents) and (2) differs from the Osaka city ordinance in that it allows for levying expenses from business operators who do not agree to the motion provided there is a 2/3 majority of business operators ((c) **non-necessity of consent**).

[19]Kadomatsu (2018, p. 9).

[20]Act No. 24 of 2005.

The amendment to the Urban Reconstruction Act is designed around the spaces defined as "residential promotion areas" and "urban function promotion areas" ((a) **authorization of area and agent**) in the Location Normalization Plan (*Ricchi Tekiseika Keikaku,* a system implemented in 2014 in the Urban Reconstruction Act[21]). This seeks to achieve the "compact city," and aims for the creation therein of such facilities as community recreation squares or streetlights to prevent crime, treating these as "facilities to be induced in the district" (*Ricchi Yudō Sokushin Shisetsu*). In this case, landowners and other rightholders in the region in question can, through unanimous agreement ((c) **necessity of consent**) and the approval of the local mayor, enter into an agreement concerning "facilities to be induced in the district" and stipulate rules on the burden of payment ((b) **costs allocation**). The local mayor can intermediate to require the participation of those persons not agreeing to participate in the agreement to do so. Unlike from the amendment to the Local Revitalization Act, the amendment to the Urban Reconstruction Act calls for the agreement of all rightholders. The key points here are that it stipulates the possibility of intermediation by the local mayor and that approved agreements still hold validity (*Shōkeikō,* succession of obligations) over persons who are not parties to the initial agreement, such as through purchase of land after the agreement is entered into. Documents by the Ministry of Land, Infrastructure, Transport, and Tourism refer to facilities for the promotion of local visits as "commons."[22]

As indicated above, area management initiatives could be interpreted as one form of avoiding the tragedy of the commons—namely, (3) **a solution through collective management**. Not only would this serve to vitalize economic activity and increase the asset value of land in the place under area management, but it would also lead to increased social capital there. Furthermore, one could expect spillover effects beyond the place under area management. At the same time, a more detailed inquiry would need to be made to identify the grounds for the "publicness" of the space as a justification for impelling those not in agreement with these activities to nevertheless cooperate.[23] Notably, due consideration must be given to whether, where area management initiatives are handled by constituent members who have equivalent interests, this results in the expulsion or exclusion of stakeholders with differing

---

[21] See Kadomatsu (2017a, p. 503) (There the author used the translation "Location Improvement Plan").

[22] http://www.mlit.go.jp/common/001220829.pdf. Accessed Mar 28, 2020.

[23] Kadomatsu (2018, p. 11). " If area management activities were to be found solely in the efforts of landowners for the purpose of promoting their asset values, it would constitute only a pursuit of private interests. (…….) The case can be made that the public nature of area management activities can be found in increasing the attractiveness of public space that is open to "many and unspecified persons", which is nothing but the classic feature of "publicness". The promotion of asset values in the area or even in the neighborhood itself cannot be recognized to be "public", unless the significance of the area is legally acknowledged, such as by its positioning in city planning. The pursuit of private interests may coexist, but these interests alone cannot be something that legitimizes public support."

interests (in particular, the risk of gentrification, when carried out in residential districts).[24]

5.3 The Tragedy of the Anticommons

5.3.1 Argument by Heller[25]

Heller's (1998) paper is written as a direct response to Hardin's theory of the "tragedy of the commons" and is entitled, "The Tragedy of the Anticommons." The "anticommons" is defined as "a property regime in which multiple owners hold effective rights of exclusion in a scarce resource." It is then subdivided into "legal" and "spatial" forms of anticommons.[26] Heller treats property rights as a "bundle of rights",[27] following Anglo-American legal tradition. The situation of legal anticommons means that "the rights of ownership, leasing, use, and so on were initially given to different owners",[28] to an asset, for example for a single piece of real estate. By contrast, the spatial anticommons refers to a context in which "each anticommons owner receives a core bundle of rights, but in too little space for the most efficient use in the given time and place."[29] This condition of anticommons invites the underuse of resources (that is, the tragedy of the anticommons). Attempting to bundle the rights after the fact reaches an impasse due to the high transactional cost and strategic behavior among parties.[30]

5.3.2 Supreme Court Judgment on the Forest Act

Heller's theory is predicated on the Anglo-American legal concept of property rights as a "bundle of rights." In Japanese law, the underlying concept differs, revolving around "standalone ownership" or "one asset, one owner." In other words, there is a single rights holder to a given asset, and the property right therein is free and exclusive.[31] From this point of view, ownership based around co-ownership (Article 249 of the Civil Code) would take on a negative connotation.

---

[24] Kadomatsu (2018, pp. 12–13).

[25] Heller (1998).

[26] Heller (1998, p. 668).

[27] Heller (1998, p. 623) n.4.

[28] Heller (1998, p. 671).

[29] Heller (1998, p. 671). "In a legal anticommons, the horizontal lines demarcate core rights of exclusion held by different owners. ...... In a spatial anticommons, by contrast, the horizontal lines demarcate the physical subdivisions of an object." (op.cit).

[30] Heller (1998, p. 659).

[31] Ishikawa(2011, p. 303).

One such case was the June 22, 1987 Supreme Court judgment[32] on the Forest Act.[33] In this case, brothers who had been given a forest plot of land from their father while he was still alive shared it equally with two stakes. They had entered a feud, and the younger brother demanded that the shared part of the forest be split up. The Civil Code states (Article 256, Paragraph 1) that any co-owner can request the split of a shared asset at any time; however, Article 186 of the Forest Act at the time did not grant such requests for the splitting of shared forests where the co-owner held a stake of less than 50%. The first appeal dismissed the younger brother's claim on the grounds of the above law, but the Supreme Court held that Article 186 of the Forest Act was a restriction on property rights that did not conform to standards of public welfare and violated Article 29, Paragraph 2 of the constitution, so it reversed the original judgment.

There are various theoretical dimensions to this ruling (an oft-cited issue is that at the time the forest became the shared property of the brothers, it had already been subject to the restrictions of Article 186 of the Forest Act, bringing into question why the brother would emphasize that his property rights were being "restricted" by the law),[34] but for our purposes, we will focus on the opinion of the court with respect to the sharing system and the demand to split up the shared asset.

> Article 186 of the Forest Act denies the right to seek partitioning provided for in Article 256, Paragraph 1 of the Civil Code[35] to a co-owner or owners with less than one half of the total value of the holding (including several co-owners with less than one half of the total value of their combined holdings). First, the Court will examine the legislative intent and purposes of Article 256 of the Civil Code. Co-ownership is for more than one person to jointly own an object. and each co-owner has a certain share of the right to own. Co-owners are not connected to each other for any special purpose except for their mutual relationship of owning something jointly. Because owners of shares in co-ownership mutually control each other, sometimes adequate consideration is not given to the use or improvement of their common property, compared to a case of single ownership. Also, disagreements and conflicts are likely to emerge between co-owners concerning the management of or changes in the property. Once a disagreement or conflict emerges, the management or changes regarding the jointly owned property may be impaired and the economic value thereof may not be fully realized. In order to avoid such impairment, and to protect a co-owner's right to control the property freely and fully realize its economic utility, the said article enables each co-owner to seek a partitioning of the jointly owned property. Furthermore, the said article sets a limit on the duration within which co-owners may conclude a contract not to partition their property, and guarantees each co-owner the right to have the jointly owned property partitioned by not recognizing the effect of the contract of prohibiting partitioning beyond the above period of time. Thus, the right to seek a partition of the jointly owned property has been developed to serve the above public objectives by enabling each co-owner to shift to a single ownership which is the basic form of ownership in modern society and has been recognized in the Civil Code as an attribute of co-ownership along with the freedom to dispose of a share in co-ownership.

---

[32]Supreme Court Judgment (Grand Bench) Apr.22, 1987 Minshu 41(3):408.

[33]*Shinrin Hō* (Act No. 249 of 1951).

[34]Annen (1995).

[35]Mimpō (Act No. 89 of 1896).

The ruling thus resulted in the interpretation that (1) given that the co-ownership produces a relationship in which the respective stakes restrict each other by their nature, therefore preventing the economic value of the asset from being realized, and (2) if treating sole ownership as the inherent form of ownership in modern society, a state of co-ownership is a transitional state that must eventually revert to sole ownership through the exercise of a right to split the asset.

(1) bears similarity to Heller's concept of the legal anticommons insofar as the way in which multiple rights holders can restrict the use, revenue generation, and disposal of an asset by other rights holders, leading to underuse. However, in the legal anticommons, multiple rights holders retain rights over fragmented parts of an asset, while in a state of co-ownership, multiple parties hold a "stake" in a single right.

The reason Article 186 of the Forest Act denies requests for a split is to maintain stable operation of the forest and prevent its fragmentation. The Supreme Court stated the following, indicating that there was no rational relationship between the legislative intent of the scheme and the restrictions in that article.

> The Forest Act excludes application of the provision of the Civil Code regarding the co-ownership to the extent that a co-owner (or co-owners) with less than half the total value of shares is not allowed to seek a partitioning of the jointly owned forest: but in all other instances the above provision on co-ownership clearly applies. However, when co-owners, particularly two co-owners with an equal share of the total value, disagree or have a conflict concerning the management or a change in the jointly owned property, each co-owner may engage only in preservation of the jointly owned forest under Article 252, proviso of the Law, and may not manage or change the jointly owned property. This may cause the devastation of the said forest. As stated above, Article 256, paragraph 1 of the Law was set up to solve this type of situation. A consequence of excluding by Article 186 of the Forest Act an application of the above provision of the Civil Code to a co-owner (or owners) of the forest with less than half the total value of the shares would merely invite a perpetuation of the above conditions, and would not help in stabilizing the management of the forest. This would clearly involve the absence of a rational relationship between the legislative objectives in Article 186 of the Forest Law and the denial in the same article to a co-owner of a forest with less than half the total value of the shares the right to have the forest divided.

Does this mean that resolving the legal anticommons produced through co-ownership requires splitting up the rights into individual ownership? Would that suffice? That is not likely the case. Let us take stock of the issues once again in light of this point.

5.3.3 *Owner-Unknown Land and the Legal Anticommons*

In Japan today, a growing social issue is that of large plots of land that are "owner unknown."[36] Some estimates suggest that 20% of Japan's landmass is owner unknown. One major factor responsible for this is the situation of legal anticommons after the inheritance.

[36] Cf. Harding (2018), Yoshihara (2015), Yohihara (2016).

According to the Japanese Civil Code, upon the death of a decedent, the estate is shared by all the heirs. This state of co-ownership will continue until the partition procedure is completed. If the heirs do not dare to take the procedure, this situation may continue for generations and the number of the heirs will multiply.

A case that is often cited is the 2013 incident of a municipality attempting to obtain a mere 192 square meter plot of land to construct a road; the rights to the land had not been re-registered since its inheritance in 1948, and the co-owners to the plot had proliferated to some 150 people, each of which had to be individually contacted.[37]

The legal anticommons caused by inheritance produces vast transaction costs that impede the use of public land and its reconstruction after disasters. We could safely describe this as "underuse." "Owner unknown" land also represents problems in terms of proper management of agricultural land and forests.

However, this does not imply that only allowing a split of the land, the solution implied by the above Forest Act Judgment of the Supreme Court, would perforce lead to a resolution of the legal anticommons discussed above.

Firstly, heirs, who are shared holders to a plot of land, can legally request a split of the inheritance at any time. If this does not occur, it is because of the transactional costs required for the split (such as registration license tax, consulting with a judicial scrivener, conferring on the split, etc.). As the asset value of land in Japan has dropped, the costs of obtaining a split-up of land exceed the potential benefits that would accrue from the land, so these processes are left unpursued and the land is not split up. In other words, underuse in this case is not only the logical **conclusion** of the legal anticommons, but also its **cause**. (1). The transactional costs and underuse associated with land—more accurately, we may not talk about "underuse" at this stage, because the term implies that the resources are not being used economically effectively,[38] but here economic demand for land itself has gone down—produce the legal anticommons, and (2) the legal anticommons increases the transactional costs, (3) inviting a **negative feedback loop of underuse** in which the land cannot be used even where there is economic demand. Where the split itself carries transaction costs, unless the division of those costs among parties is discussed, the legal anticommons cannot be resolved.

Secondly, even supposing a split resolves the legal anticommons, there may be cases where a spatial anticommons exists. This leads to the property rights becoming too fragmented and being unable to be used effectively. The issue of "owner

---

[37]Cf. The Tokyo Foundation (2014, pp. 20–21).

[38]As a matter of fact, the "underuse" by Heller is conceptually inseparable from the cost-benefit analysis. "Searching for an optimum between overuse and underuse sets us on the contested path of modern regulation of risk, an inquiry that starts with economic analysis but quickly implicates our core beliefs… I note this difficult topic to show that finding the optimum requires the idea of underuse and that this new word in turn transforms the meaning of overuse. Overuse no longer just means using a resource more than an ordinary amount. The possibility of underuse reorients policy making from relatively simple either-or choices to the more contentious trade-offs that make up modern regulation of risk." Heller (2013, pp. 15–16). Cf. Heller (2008, pp. 35–36).

unknown" land on so-called "shared private roads" is indicative of this problem.[39] In Japan, buildings must abut the road; in order to meet this requirement, there are cases where adjacent owners provide their private land as a common road and have it designated by a government agency as such. When the owners of a "shared private road" of this nature become unknown for some reason, repairs to the pavement and updates to infrastructure like water mains and sewer pipes are impeded, leading to the tragedy of the anticommons. Where these roads are shared by adjacent owners, in addition to being classed as "joint private roads," they may be referred to in some cases as "reciprocal cross-driveways." This is where the plot of the private roads consists of multiple sections, with the owners of the adjacent residential plots each owning the respective sections, and mutually allowing each other to use them. For reciprocal cross-driveways, the ownership rights are intentionally fragmented at the time of the creation of the road, creating conditions where the respective owners cannot obstruct each other's use. In this case, there is no legal anticommons, but inability to contact the individual owners of the fragmented road may produce a spatial anticommons.

5.3.4 Solutions to the Tragedy of the Anticommons

5.3.4.1 Tasks Facing Solution Through Property Rights

What measures might we take to address the tragedy of the anticommons in cases where owners are unknown?

Firstly, when this issue is attempted to be resolved by property law and the split-up is resolved ("solution through property rights" (supra 1.2)), there is then a further need to discuss who is to bear the transaction costs associated. When it further creates spatial anticommons, we should discuss how to bring them together and aggregate the fragmented ownership rights.[40,41]

Secondly, the countermeasures to take must be distinguished based on what sort of issue the "owner unknown" land has produced and in what sense it represents a tragedy of the anticommons. Gakuto Takamura classifies underuse into two types: (a) **underuse from a holistic perspective** (not disturbing neighbors, but where the use of the real estate is inefficient for the plot in question) and (b) **underuse infringing on neighbors** (insufficient management creates large externalities that infringe on neighbors).[42]

---

[39] See the Ministry of Justice (2018).

[40] E.g. proposal of Land Assembly Districts (Heller and Hills (2008)).

[41] Additionally, there is also a question of how to produce the information on the owners and whether one may use/distribute the information.

[42] Takamura (2015, p. 67).

5.3.4.2 Measures against negative externalities (neighborhood perspective)

Let the owner bear the costs

Examples of case b) would be a vacant home where the owner is unknown, inviting decay of a shared forest or farmland and causing a negative externality to the neighboring residents. There is therefore significance to clearly delineating a rule here that states that the owner is responsible for the cost of these negative externalities. This would create an incentive where the owner would take appropriate measures, such as disposing of the land, before it reaches a state of "owner unknown." However, this strategy would not be effective in cases where, at the time of inheritance, there is no demand for the plot. Furthermore, if the plot has already slipped into a state of "owner unknown," and there is a duty to make payment, the owner may hesitate to voluntarily provide that information, which would in turn further inhibit a resolution of the problem.

Compulsory Measures

(1) Unoccupied House Act—specified vacant homes

One means of handling (b) negative externalities would involve imposing compulsory measures. The Act on Special Measures for the Promotion of Measures for Unoccupied Houses hereafter, ("Unoccupied House Act")[43] defines "specified vacant homes" producing pronounced negative externalities to neighboring residents and employs measures where, following warnings/administrative guidance to the owner, the property can ultimately be removed by "subrogation". Where it is unable to ascertain the land owner without negligence on the part of the municipality, it is possible to employ a legal scheme of "summary subrogation" by public notice.

(2) Forest Act—forests requiring thinning or otherwise

Further, the Forest Act allows, for "forests requiring thinning" (that is, those left unattended and requiring immediate thinning or preservation), the local mayor to notify and recommend the owner of the forest to take measures. Where the owner does not accede to the recommendation, they can then be advised to engage in consultation for the transfer or establishment of the rights of the owner or third parties. Where the parties fail to reach agreement, the prefectural governor may issue a "ruling" (*Saitei*) in order to establish the minimum required ownership and/or usage rights for periodic thinning, etc. A 2011 amendment to the Forest Act states that, where the owners are unknown, a public notice can be used for the above ruling over the compulsory establishment of ownership/usage rights.

---

[43] *Akiya Tō Taisaku no Suishin ni Kansuru Tokubetsu Sochihō* (Act. No. 127 of 2014). See Chap. 1 of this book.

5.3.4.3 Measures against ineffective use (holistic perspective)

What would happen when there is no negative externality but there is some form of demand for the plot of land, which is being impeded by its current condition? This case, where an underuse from a holistic perspective (the above (a)) occurs, could be subdivided into those where (i) the intended purpose of use is inherent to the characteristics of the plot of land or (ii) the intended purpose of use is completely external to the plot of land.

Establishing Purposes inherent to the characteristics of the plot of the land

(1) Forest Act—right to use another's land for the purpose of forest management

According to the Forest Act (Article 50 para 1), those who remove timber from the forest or build forest roads or other equipment necessary for forest management can ask for the approval of the prefectural governor to ask for consultation to use another's land if there is no alternative. Where the parties fail to reach agreement, the governor may issue a ruling to establish the right to use the land. The 2011 amendment made it possible to proceed the process even when the owner is unknown, using public hearing, public notice and deposition. In this case, the existence of negative externality is not the prerequisite, and the compulsory setting of the right to use may be analogous to expropriation. On the other hand, indispensability of the use of another's land is mainly due to topographic constraint and the necessity of forest management is inherent to the nature of forest.

(2) Cropland Act[44]—right to use unused cropland for the promotion of use

Another example of the measures against the above (i) (the intended purpose of use is inherent to the characteristics of the plot of land) is the system for obtaining right to use for unused cropland. The Cropland Act employs a set of "ruling" measures that resemble those employed in the Forest Act; these measures are used by the Institutes for the Intermediary Management of Agricultural Lands (Agricultural Land Bank) to obtain usage rights for fallow land. Unlike the Forest Act, in the case of fallow agricultural land, even if it does not necessarily produce negative externalities on neighbors, the law allows for the obtaining of usage rights "where it is deemed necessary and appropriate for the promotion of use of the land for agricultural purposes." The above chooses to focus on the efficient use of resources. This system can be used even in cases where the owners are unknown. If the agricultural commission is unable to ascertain the land owner without negligence on its part, the commission may publicly notice the fallow land. After 6 months from the public notice, the Agricultural Land Bank may apply for the ruling of the governor to obtain usage rights.

---

[44] *Nōchi Hō* (Act No. 229 of 1952).

This system does not presuppose the existence of negative externalities—to be sure, there may be abstract risk of such in unused cropland. Compared to forests, there is less topographic constraint. However, at least in the case of cropland (and also for forest land), the intended purpose of use for the plot is legally fixed and the specific nature of what it would mean to make "efficient use of the resources" of the plot of land is to a certain extent clear. The Cropland Act stipulates that "persons who have ownership of or the right of lease of agricultural land, or any other right to use and derive profit from cropland must ensure that cropland is used in an agriculturally-appropriate and efficient manner) (Article 2-2).

(3) Special clauses for "co-owner unknown land"—measures against legal anti-commons

Recent legislations stipulate special measures to establish the right to use in the cases where the co-owners are unknown. The 2016 amendment of the Forest Act provides for the right of a co-owner of the forest to apply to the local mayor to take the necessary to take steps to find the other co-owners whose name/whereabouts are unknown. If no one appears after the public notice, the co-owner who made the application may ask for a ruling by the governor to let her obtain the right to use timbers and lands of the other co-owners' until the next cutting age.

Under the newly enacted Forest Management Act[45] in 2018, the municipalities may lay down a Forest Management Right Aggregation Plan, obtain the right to use from the owners and conduct municipal management or let a specific private enterprise manage the forest. Under the Act, the requirement for the Forest Management Right Aggregation Plan is made easier for the case when the co-owners are not known. A similar scheme was introduced for agricultural land in the 2018 amendment of Agricultural Management Framework Reinforcement Act.[46]

Purposes external to the characteristics of the plot of the land

What occurs, then, when the intended use for the plot of land is (ii) purely external to the characteristics of the plot of the land?

(1) "Unknown Adjudication" System in the Expropriation of Land Act

The typical case of the external purpose is, of course, the Expropriation of Land Act,[47] which allows for compulsory obtaining of ownership rights against the will of the owner. It should be obvious that the same compulsory process applies to cases where the owner is unknown. For these cases, the Expropriation of Land Act employs a system of "unknown adjudication."

---

[45] *Shinrin Keiei Kanri Hō* (Act No. 35 of 2018).

[46] *Nogyō Keiei Kiban Kyōka Sokushin Hō* (Act No. 65 of 1980).

[47] Act No. 219 of 1951.

(2) 2018 Unclaimed Land Act

The Special Measures Act on Facilitation of Use of Land where the Owner is Unknown[48] (hereafter the "Unclaimed Land Act"), enacted in June 2018, defines "unclaimed land" as "the plot of land where all or part of the owners are unknown, even after the reasonable effort has been made by the method stipulated by the Cabinet Order" (Article 2 para.1). The law stipulates (a) the special procedure for the land expropriation in case of unclaimed land and (b) the scheme to establish right to use for the "undertakings for the promotion of welfare of the community".

(a) Special procedure for the land expropriation.

In the case of the "specified unclaimed land", where there is no building and it is not being used for business or for other special purposes (Article 2, Paragraph 2), the Unclaimed Land Act makes it possible to expropriate land by the "ruling" of the prefectural governor, different from the normal procedure of "expropriation adjudication" by the prefectural Expropriation Commission. Since the Expropriation Commission is a council system organization that includes outside experts, the meeting schedule is limited, which acts as a bottle neck for the expropriation procedure. This special procedure is legitimated, so the government says, because it is easy to calculate compensation in the case of specified unclaimed land and one can ascertain that there is no rightholders' objection to the compensation using public notice procedure.

(b) Right of use for the undertakings for the promotion of welfare of the community.

"Undertakings for the promotion of welfare of the community" *(Chiiki Fukuri Zōshin Jigyō)* is defined as the undertakings for the "promotion of common welfare or convenience of community residents etc." and the Unclaimed Land Act enumerates roads, parking lots, public parks etc. (Article 2, para 3). An entrepreneur may apply for the ruling of the governor to establish the right of use for unclaimed land for the purpose of such undertakings. The longest term for the right of use is 10 years. Even when the project does not belong to the undertakings enumerated under the Expropriation of Land Act (Article 3), establishing the right of use is possible, albeit the ownership transaction is impossible.

The Unclaimed Land Act thus makes it possible to compulsorily establish the right of use for unclaimed land for the purpose of undertakings that "may not have enough public welfare nature that would legitimize compulsory ownership transfer by land expropriation but do have a certain degree of public nature such as promotion of welfare or convenience of community residents". How can we evaluate such a scheme?

As stated in 1.1. there are two frames of reasoning as a basis for justifying the property rights system: (1) protection of personal freedoms and (2) greater efficiency

[48] *Shoyūsha Fumei Tochi no Riyō no Enkatsuka Tō ni Kansuru Tokubetsu Sochi Hō* (Act No. 49 of 2018).

in the use of the resources that enhances the welfare of society as a whole. It goes without saying that the need to protect land ownership rights from the point of view of (1) would already have been quite diluted in cases of unclaimed land. In addition, there is a need for some state interventions to cope with the situation of legal or spatial anticommons from the perspective of (2).

Which type or degree of state interventions is desirable and how can they be legitimized, then? First, one may focus on the decrease of objective/subjective value of the asset itself. Katsumi Yoshida names property whose value is low and which does not meet the cost of maintenance as a "negative asset". For such a negative asset, there is an imbalance between the cost of detailed cautious procedures for defending the rights and interests of landowners under the Expropriation of Land Act and the actual smallness of the interest of defended landowners. Such imbalances may legitimate the special procedure of land expropriation, skipping the procedures of the Expropriation Commission.[49]

Second, one may legitimize the intervention on the basis of the presumed will of the unknown owner. Since the unclaimed land does not attract the owner's attention any more, one can presume that the owner does not object to the use by other person, if the contact were possible.

Third, how should we evaluate the scheme to establish the right of use of land in comparison to compulsory land ownership transfer? The separation of the right to use and the ownership has a potential to lead to the solution through collective management (1.2). Some evaluate the scheme of the Agricultural Land Bank as a step that leads to a management system as "a modern form of *Gesamteigentum*" (a concept in German law), making possible collective management of the cropland as commons. The "undertakings for the promotion of welfare of the community" scheme in the Unclaimed Land Act does not seek joint management. However, the scheme of "certification of civic green space", introduced by the 2017 amendment of the Urban Green Space Conservation Act,[50] allows for the short-term use of vacant city lots by citizens or local groups through the coordination of the municipality.[51] The latter would be an example of solution through collective management. A similar system of "the plan to promote establishment of rights for use of unutilized or low utilized land" *(Tei Mi Riyōchi Tochi Kenri Settei Tō Sokushin Keikaku)* was introduced in the Urban Reconstruction Act by the 2018 amendment.

There is criticism against the system of establishing the right to use in the Unclaimed Land Act. While the law obligates restoration to the original state after the land use term has expired, such criticism argues that this obligation would limit the range of economically feasible projects for the legal scheme and thus acquiring ownership is necessary. Some also argue that the law should abandon the requirement of "publicness" and allow municipalities to rent or sell unclaimed land on behalf of the owner to anyone who has interest in using the land, even for purely "private" purposes. To be sure, if we do not expect anything from the direction toward future

[49]Yoshida (2018).

[50]*Toshi Ryokuchi Hō* (Act No. 72 of 1973).

[51]Takamura (2018, p. 47).

collective management of commons by establishing the right to use, it may be more natural to forget about the "publicness" of the purpose. So the prospect to the "third solution" to the tragedy of commons is the turning point.

The legal scheme of establishing the right of use has the possibility to lead to future collective management on the one hand, but may lead to a complex legal relationship as a conduit for legal anticommons on the other hand. In my view, the choice between three solutions to the tragedy of commons—property law, rule-setting and collective management—should be a flexible and strategical judgment on case-by-case and trial-and-error basis. A doctrinal approach with a lexical priority rule may not be most productive.

References

Annen J (1995) Kempō ga Zaisanken wo Hogosuru Koto no Imi (The meaning of constitutional protection of property rights). In: Hasebe Y (ed) Reedinguzu Gendai no Kempō. Nihonhyoronsha, Tokyo, pp 137–153

Hardin G (1968) The tragedy of the commons. Science 162:1243–1248

Heller M (1998) The tragedy of the anticommons: property in the transition from marx to markets. Harv Law Rev 111:621–688

Harding R (2018) Japan's lost lands: why a fifth of the nation's territory is worthless. Financial Times Jan. 18, 2018. https://www.ft.com/content/3aaa626e-f61f-11e7-8715-e94187b3017e. Accessed 24 Mar 2020

Heller M (2008) The gridlock economy: how too much ownership wrecks markets stops innovation and costs lives. Basic Books, New York

Heller M (2013) The tragedy of the anticommons: a concise introduction and Lexicon. Mod Law Rev 76(1):6–25

Heller M, Hills R (2008) Land assembly districts. Harv Law Rev 121(6):1465–1527

Ishikawa K (2011) Hōseido no Honshitsu to Hireigensoku no Tekiyō (The essence of legal institution and application of proportionality principle). In, "Purosesu Enshū Kempō, 4th edn. Shinzansha, Tokyo, pp 291–320

Kadomatsu N (2017a) A misinterpretation or a productive diversion? -the rise and fall of the "relationship of reciprocal interchangeability" concept and the possibility of reception of a legal interpretation. In: Weaver RL, Hofmann HCH, Huang C, Friedland SI (eds) Comparative perspectives on administrative procedure. Carolina Academic Press, Durham, pp 105–127

Kadomatsu N (2017b) Legal management of urban space in Japan and the role of the judiciary. In: Rose-Ackerman S et al (eds) Comparative administrative law, 2nd edn. Edward Elgar, Cheltenham, pp 497–512

Kadomatsu N (2018) Inclusion and seclusion in area management activities. Zeitschrift für Japanisches Recht (Journal of Japanese Law) 45:5–15

Ministry of Justice, The (2018) Shoyūsha Fumei Shidō e no Taiō Gaidorain (A guideline for measures toward owner-unknown shared private roads). http://www.moj.go.jp/content/001266072.pdf. Accessed 28 Mar 2020

Ostrom E (1990) Governing the commons: the evolution of institutions for collective action. Cambridge University Press, Cambridge

Rose CM (1986) The comedy of the commons: custom, commerce, and inherently public property. Univ Chic Law Rev 53(3):711–781

Suga Y (2008) Komonzu no Kigeki (Comedy of the Commons). In: Inoue M (ed) Komonzu Ron no Chōsen. Shinyōsha, Tokyo, pp 2–19

Takamura G (2012) Komonzu kara no Toshi Saisei (Urban regeneration beginning from commons). Mineruba Shobō, Kyoto
Takamura G (2015) Kashō Riyō Jidai ni okeru Shoyūken Ron Saiko (Rethinking property law theory in an era of underuse). Hoshakaigaku 81:64–75
Takamura G (2018) Gendai Toshihō Ron to Toshi Komonzu Kenkyū—Renketsu no tameno Shiron (A Thought on Combining the Theory of Contemporary Urban Law and Urban Commons Studies). In: Kurumizawa Y et al (eds) Gendai Toshihō no Kadai to Tembō. Nihonhyōronsha, Tokyo, pp 29–52
Tokyo Foundation, The (2014) Kokudo no Fumeika, Shizōka no Kiki (The crisis of national land becoming owner-unknown and dead storage). https://www.tkfd.or.jp/files/product/2013–06.pdf. Accessed 28 Mar 2020
Yoshida K (2018) Shoyūsha Fumei Tochi Mondai to Tochi Shoyūken Ron (Unclaimed Land Problem and the Theory of Property Rights). Hōritsu Jihō 90(9):68–77
Yoshihara S (2015) Property Laws Hindering Disaster Recovery
https://www.tkfd.or.jp/en/research/detail.php?id=594. Accessed 24 Mar 2020
Yoshihara S (2016) Japan's "Missing landowners": legal framework for land ownership inadequate to cope with aging, depopulation. https://www.tkfd.or.jp/en/research/detail.php?id=17. Accessed 24 Mar 2020

The manufacturer's authorised representative in the EU is Springer Nature Customer Service Centre GmbH, Europaplatz 3, 69115 Heidelberg, Germany. If you have any concerns regarding our products, please contact ProductSafety@springernature.com

Printed and bound by CPI Group (UK) Ltd, Croydon, CR0 4YY
01/10/2026
02226351-0010